D0680773

The
SHAUN
CASSIDY
SCRAPBOOK

AN ILLUSTRATED BIOGRAPHY

By

Connie Berman

TEMPO BOOKS
GROSSET & DUNLAP, Inc., Publishers
New York, N.Y. 10010
A Filmways Company

THE SHAUN CASSIDY SCRAPBOOK

ISBN: 0-448-14738-6
A Tempo Books Original
Tempo Books is registered in the U.S. Patent Office

Printed in the United States of America

The Shaun Cassidy Scrapbook

1

If stardom is like a dream come true, then Shaun Cassidy is having the most fabulous dream of a lifetime!

Little more than a year ago, few people had ever heard of Shaun Cassidy. Now, his record albums are selling in the millions, his concerts are jam-packed, his songs punctuate the radio stations several times a day, and he's also starring in the popular "Hardy Boys" television series. His well-scrubbed, sweet-faced good looks are on the covers of countless magazines as well as posters and tee-shirts. Shaun is America's newest teen idol, the dream pop singer; millions of teenagers would agree to that. He's riding the crest of an immense wave of popularity that only seems to swell as time goes by. A true multimedia star, Shaun is really happening, and there's no one who enjoys it more than the talented young man himself. He's taken the entertainment world and the hearts of an endless number of swooning girls by storm.

Today, the name Shaun is as much a household word as Fonzie or Barbarino. Yet, unlike Fonzie or Barbarino, Shaun is a different kind of teen idol. He's young and earnest and basically the sort of guy we would all like to know. He's a star but also the nice boy-next-door all rolled up into one fetching package.

Despite his unique status as pop idol, Shaun is really a lot like other teenagers, which makes him all the more endearing.

By day, Shaun toils away as younger brother Joe Hardy on the juvenile gumshoe series "The Hardy Boys," along with Parker Stevenson. He has probably achieved more fame from his astoundingly successful music career which began in Europe some two years ago and really caught on in America last year. Both of Shaun's albums, "Shaun Cassidy" and "Born Late," have gone platinum—record company lingo for selling more than a million copies—and his singles "Da Doo Ron Ron," "That's Rock n Roll," and "Hey Deanie" have all skyrocketed to the top of the charts. The second album heralded the debut of Shaun as a composer too, since he wrote five of the ten songs on the LP.

The fact that Shaun has become a successful show business performer is really no surprise, considering his background. The shock comes from the dizzying pace at which his career took off and propelled into ultra-high gear. In less than a year, Shaun went from a relative unknown to one of the most popular entertainers in the country. That's no mean feat for a guy who isn't yet out of his teens; just a bare nineteen years of age and already a millionaire.

Shaun's roots are deeply imbedded in show business, therefore, he never lacked an example for becoming a star. His half brother is former "Partridge Family" star and ex-teen heartthrob David Cassidy, who reigned over the world of pop music in the early 1970s; much as Shaun does now. Shaun's mother is musical comedy star, Oscar-award winning actress and also "Partridge Family" veteran Shirley Jones, who broke into show business at an early age herself. His father is the late highly gifted Broadway and TV actor and singer Jack Cassidy. Yet, Shaun's heady success is really his own doing. Sure, it was helpful to be who he was, to have that set of parents and gain a foot in the door, but his ascension to the top is because of his own determination, drive, and vast store of talent.

"I'm loving every minute of what is happening to me now," exults Shaun, clearly relishing his fame. "I can't imagine doing anything else!" Of course, there are moments, especially when he is robbed of his privacy, that Shaun envies the more traditional and more normal life of some of his pals from high school —the ones who went off to college, and the ones who did not enter show business. But then he grins and says, "I've made my choice . . . A lot of my friends have gone off to college to pursue careers. I just happen to be lucky enough to be pursuing mine right now."

He has also said, clearly aware of the drawbacks of his role as teen idol supreme. "It really gets to me sometimes. But I wanted success and this is part of it."

Shaun's level-headed attitude is also evident in the way he talks about show business. He's seen through the glamorous trappings, the razzle-dazzle, and the glitter to the hard facts of what life in the public eye is really like. He knows it's no fairy-tale land, but a business just like any other.

Above all, Shaun is a cool professional. "I want to keep my options open. In every facet of show business, there are dangers. . . . I see show business as a business," he sums up.

Whenever a new teen idol emerges out of the depths of anonymity; whenever an unknown becomes a hot new star, as Shaun has done, there's always the question of how long he will last. There are always new people in the wings, would-be heartthrobs who are only all too willing to take Shaun's place as prince of the teen world. With his kind of talent, and moreover, his keen sense of what it means to be a performer and how to run his own life, it looks like Shaun will reign over his worshipful public for a long time.

Hard-working yet calm, bright and intelligent yet fun-loving, Shaun says, "I think success is a question of not taking yourself too seriously."

Of course, that attitude is fine for Shaun, but the rest of America take their heroes very seriously, and right now, especially among teens, Shaun is number one!

2

There are times that Shaun Cassidy must wonder—where would I be today if my mother had been a housewife, and my father had been a businessman, and I had grown up in, say St. Louis? It's hard to figure out what the answer to that question would be, because Shaun is a vastly talented young man. He hasn't gained so much prominence just because of who his parents are—to come as far as he has come, takes much more than that. Shaun would be the first to admit that having parents who were both well-known in show business helped him get an easier foothold when he started.

Still he feels that when one has a famous legacy as he does, it can be as much a disadvantage as an advantage. He feels that people tend to judge much more harshly; they're more apt to be critical and more apt to downgrade one's talents. That's why he feels, "You've got to work to be better than average all the time."

Then too, Shaun's going into show business was a way of proving himself as a person and finding his own identity. From the beginning, he remembers, he was known as Shirley Jones' son, Jack Cassidy's son, then later as David Cassidy's half brother. He wanted to be just Shaun. He recalls being hurt when friends or acquaintances would introduce him as "the son of Shirley Jones." The first autograph he ever signed was because of whom his mother was. "It was so long ago, and it wasn't because I was Shaun Cassidy, it was because I was Shirley Jones' son. I do remember it was when my mom was on the road doing a show and someone asked me to sign my name. I was about four or five at the time."

The pretty blond woman whom Shaun calls "Mom" and whom audiences know as an Oscar award-winning actress and topnotch singer, was born in a small town called Smithton, Pennsylvania, on March 31, 1934. Smithton, with its population of 800, provided the classic, small-home-town setting for Shirley's youth and set up her old-fashioned, natural values. From the beginning, a career in show business loomed across the horizon. Shirley was named for Shirley Temple, the curly-headed tot performer of movies. Her father, whose last name was indeed Jones, ran the local brewery, called Stoney's Beer, which her grandmother owned.

In a way, Shirley, who was an only child, had the kind of Pollyanna childhood and early success that are right out of those fluffy musicals of the 1930s—the kind where small town girl makes it big. There were no tragedies, no poverty-stricken youth, no heartbreaking melodrama. It is a real Cinderella story for an actress who could be a Cinderella herself.

Early on, Shirley discovered that she had a talent for singing. "I could sing as far back as I can remember. My mother used to stand me up at parties and have me sing for the guests." She sang at church, at school, at camp, everywhere, since she was about three or four.

Despite her image today as a nice, ladylike woman, Shirley recalls that there were periods when as a child, she acted like a spoiled brat.

"I was a happy child but I was very difficult. . . . I was an only child . . . I had a very strong will and wouldn't be held down . . . I would have temper tantrums, hit my head against the wall, scream in defiance.

"I was impossible. My mother spanked me every day but it seemed to do no good. I would fight with boys, and come home with my clothes torn—mind you, this was all before I was eight. I had a great amount of energy and used it to do whatever I wanted. When I couldn't get my way, I used to scream and cry. My mother would try putting me in my room. That didn't work either . . . Every day was a constant fight."

One area where Shirley urged her parents to give in was in music lessons. When a camp counselor perceived how much talent she had, he suggested that Shirley have voice lessons, and she asked and asked until her parents agreed. Not that it was a simple matter. Shirley had to be chauffered to vocal lessons in Pittsburgh, which was about 30 miles away from Smithton, three times a week, by her compliant mother. When she graduated from high school in 1952, she used her singing talent to enter the Miss Pittsburgh contest in the Miss America pageant. After she was named the winner, all thoughts of continuing her education at St. Mary's College for Girls, stopped. Shirley had her sights on the national pageant, but she never got to the Atlantic City contest. Despite that crystalline voice and her wholesome, apple-cheeked beauty, Shirley was runner-up in the Miss Pennsylvania pageant and lost out on the state title. In 1953, determined Shirley, just 19 (Shaun's age now), armed herself with $245 in savings and headed for New York. It was a journey made with the grudging assent of her parents.

It was there that the magic started happening for Shirley, just like in the movies. She tried out for a part as a nurse in the chorus of *South Pacific,* then running on Broadway. Almost like in a script, the director who heard her sing urged that she try out for Richard Rodgers who was casting for the movie version of *Oklahoma* at the time. So she sang for Rodgers.

Shirley landed the part of the nurse in the *South Pacific* chorus, then went on to play the lead of Juliet in the road company of *Me and Juliet.* While traveling with that musical, she tested opposite Gordon Mac-Crae, for the role of Laurie. In less than a year after she first sang in the *South Pacific* tryout, Shirley Jones, new girl in town, had won the coveted role of Laurie in *Oklahoma.* She hadn't even guessed that she had won the part, when one day her agent called her and said, "Hello, Laurie." No wonder a friend, speaking of Shirley, says, "She doesn't know what it is to connive to get the breaks."

That was the first in a succession of nice-girl parts for Shirley, who seemed tailor made for the girl-next-door type. She next won the lead in the movie version of *Carousel* and consequently played opposite such big-name stars in movies as James Stewart, Glenn Ford, Henry Fonda, David Niven, Marlon Brando, and Pat Boone. Her performance in *Elmer Gantry* with Burt Lancaster won her an Oscar, and proved that Shirley could play a variety of roles.

It was while Shirley was rehearsing for a Department of State company of *Oklahoma* that was to tour Europe in 1955, that she met the man who was to be the great love of her life—Jack Cassidy. A handsome and dashing actor with a healthy dose of Irish charm, Cassidy was to play Curley, opposite Shirley's rendition of Laurie. The two were in love on-screen and soon found themselves falling in love off-screen as well.

They returned to the States after their tour and both were determined to work things out. Their careers, however, kept them apart—Shirley was slated to appear in the film *Carousel* and had to go to Maine for on-location filming. Jack was acting on stage in Philadelphia. After a few months of mad commuting to see each other, and after Jack had been able to obtain a divorce, they were finally married.

The wedding took place almost on the spur of the moment. Jack and Shirley decided to become man and wife only three weeks before they actually married. They didn't even have time to send out invitations, only to phone their family and friends. They were married on August 6, 1956, at the New Church of Jerusalem in Cambridge, Massachusetts; about a year after they had first met on the *Oklahoma* tour. Shirley and Jack were costarring together at the time, at the Cambridge Drama Festival, in a play called *The Beggar's Opera,* which interestingly enough featured them as man and wife. Shirley looked radiant at her wedding, in a beautiful long white gown with full peau de soie skirt.

Those who knew her well said that Shirley's choice of Jack as a bridegroom proved that she was certainly more complex than the girl-next-door image commonly depicted of her in the press. "You can see that there is something more than the sweet young thing in

Shirley by her taste in men," says a long-time friend. Jack was a sophisticated, man of the world, and the marriage said that there was a lot about Shirley the public didn't guess.

Jack Cassidy, one of Broadway's most accomplished performers was born in New York City, on March 5, 1925. Unlike Shirley, he came from a poor and underprivileged background, where he was forced to hold a succession of some fifteen various jobs, while still a youngster, to bring money home to his folks. He finally dropped out of high school at the age of sixteen, to make his debut on Broadway. He then went on to appear in a variety of American and European stage roles, winning Tony awards and acclaim as a singer and actor of great flair and talent. His first wife was an actress named Evelyn Ward whom he married in 1948, and with whom he had a son named David. They were divorced in 1955.

After Shirley and Jack were married, she held back on her career to spend more time with him and to become a mother. The couple embarked on a nightclub tour in which they sang and danced and did parodies side by side. They appeared all over the country, often with baby Shaun in tow. They also performed together in television and summer stock. The nightclub act included renditions from Rodgers and Hammerstein and other favorite Broadway hits through the years, including the shows that Jack had been in.

Shirley clearly flourished as a wife and mother and certainly delighted in domestic chores like decorating, cooking, and baking. She became a three-time mother, and considered herself a surrogate mother to her stepson David Cassidy. She whipped up a lot of home-cooked meals and baked a lot of pies and cakes. In the process, she tried to domesticate her own free-wheeling husband, only to discover that he wasn't the type to be tamed.

Admitting once that she and Jack Cassidy were "exact opposites," Shirley recalled that, "When I first married Jack, I did my best to change him. I wanted him to be active in the PTA, Boy Scouts, and that sort of thing. But it never worked and now that I look back, I'm not sorry."

To those who questioned why, the actress who had won an Oscar and a movie career that could have escalated her to the top star of the 1960s, she would say, "My career is secondary to my husband and my children."

She once told an interviewer that, if Jack had wanted her to, she probably would have even given up her career but, she said, he loved the fact that she was working.

Shirley herself has said, "I never had a great force behind me like a lot of women in this business. I simply do the best I can. I'm not a competitor."

Almost in spite of herself, Shirley did gain fame and fortune, especially after "The Partridge Family" series, a show that really propelled her into the limelight and made her one of the country's most beloved actresses during the show's four-year reign. It gave Shirley the greatest measure of fame she had ever known in her long career.

It was during Shirley's position as mother hen of the Partridge brood that she and Jack began having marital troubles. Finally, in 1974, Shirley and Jack were divorced after eighteen years of marriage. It was a sad time for all of them, but as Shirley said, probably most of all for Jack, who felt very lonely.

Shirley started dating Marty Ingels, a former comedian who was now making several million dollars a year by signing stars to do commercial spots.

Then, in 1976, shortly before Christmas, Jack was killed in a fire in his West Hollywood apartment.

Shirley and her children were deeply shaken by his death, of course not only because he was gone, but also because of the terribly tragic way he died.

Despite her grief, Shirley tried to put her life back together again. A year later, she wed Marty Ingels, in a Jewish ceremony in the Beverly Hills Bel-Air Hotel in November 1977. Shaun was the one who gave the bride away. After the ceremony, there was a champagne reception and dinner. Shirley sang the special song that she and Marty shared called "He Touched Me." Their wedding cake decorated with pink chrysanthemums was wheeled out after that, and the couple honeymooned for several weeks in Alaska.

So it's a whole new life for Shirley and also a whole new life for her son Shaun, who's now achieving a great fame of his own and carrying on that prestigious show business family legacy.

3

A few months before their wedding in Massachusetts, in 1956, Jack Cassidy gave his bride-to-be, Shirley Jones, a very special birthday present—one that was thoughtful but would also turn out to be prescient as well. The gift was a painting of a small boy called *The Dreamer*. "If we ever have a son," Jack told his fiancee then, "I know he will look like that."

Amazingly enough, Jack's prophetic words turned out to be true. When their firstborn child, a son, arrived, he looked very much like the boy in the painting. The features of Shaun Paul Cassidy, as he was named, and those of the boy in the painting were startlingly similar, although the boy was blond and Shaun was born with tufts of dark hair. For a long time, the painting was hung in a special spot in Shirley and Jack's bedroom.

Shaun was born on a Saturday, on the 27th of September, 1958, at night. His mother gave birth to him in St. John's Hospital, in Santa Monica, California—it was the very first time Shirley had ever been in a hospital in her life. The baby weighed in at an impressive nine pounds and four ounces, which more than made up for the fact that Shaun, as with most first babies, was more than three weeks overdue. As a matter of fact, Shirley and Jack had cancelled a concert tour to await the arrival and were virtually watching the clock hands in expectation of the blessed event.

Shirley and Jack had booked an appearance together at a club in Dallas, which was supposed to take place after the baby came—had he arrived on time. When he didn't, they had to move back the opening date.

When Shaun finally did come into the world, he was the biggest baby Hollywood had ever seen. He held a sort of improvised title of heavyweight baby among the stars' children, until a son born to actress Nanette Fabray beat Shaun out by a few ounces and became the new bearer of the title.

Shaun was such a bouncing, healthy chunk of a boy that to many onlookers, at six months he seemed like a one-year-old. He was, from the start, a handsome little tyke, who appeared to favor his mother in looks. He had her features, columnists wrote, her almond eyes and round, innocent face.

Shaun was a good-natured, happy baby, who basked in the glow of the deep love and affection of two proud parents. He rarely cried. He ate heartily, and his parents couldn't keep track of his weight as he grew by leaps and bounds.

"We let him tank up and hoped he'll grow up rugged like his dad," said Shirley, shortly after Shaun was born. "And beautiful like his mother," Jack would counter.

From the beginning, Shaun displayed a disarming curiosity of the world around him and an intelligence that made him seem older than his years. He quickly learned how to spell out his name with little plastic sticks and would demonstrate this skill to every guest in the Cassidy home.

At that early age he didn't seem very impressed or caught up with the glittery world of show business, although he had toured with his parents at the age of three weeks in nightclubs. He hardly knew what the word movie star meant and scarcely realized that his own mother was indeed one of those special creatures. His world was much simpler, more down-to-earth, and unaffected than that. He would say, as a toddler, when asked what he wanted to be when he grew up, that there were three things—"A big man, a fire engine and a police car."

Sometimes Shaun would take an excursion into the world of show business with his mother or father. Occasionally Shirley would dress him up in a special outfit, and he would accompany her for the day to the set of a movie she was filming. He would go with his father on location to one of the TV shows that Jack Cassidy appeared on. However, with all the typical nonchalance of a four- or five-year-old, Shaun was not overwhelmed by all this. He much preferred to play with his toys out in the backyard.

He did like his mother's voice, and especially liked it when she sang to him at night before he went off to sleep. His favorite song was called "Go To Sleep, Little One."

Shaun also took great delight in having his father, with that rich commanding voice that he was famous for, read bedtime stories to him. "Snow White and The Seven Dwarfs" was a particular favorite, since Jack would assume a different voice for each of the dwarfs. Other nights he liked "The Three Little Pigs." One of his very favorites was "Pinocchio," the tale about the little boy whose nose grew long when he told lies. It was one of Shaun's biggest childhood thrills when his mother took him, along with his half-brother David, to the film version of that story. Shirley was appearing on the big screen herself at the time, in the film *Hollywood Melody,* but it was *Pinocchio* that young Shaun really wanted to see.

One thing that was very important to Shirley was to pass on to her son a faith in God and a deep sense of religion. Helping Shaun say his prayers at night was as much a nighttime ritual as being read a story or being sung a song. It was all part of saying goodnight and preparing for sleep.

"As soon as my son Shaun began to enjoy the routine of getting ready for bed, I began to teach him his prayers," recalls Shirley. "At first he only rocked back and forth in time with the rhythm of the verse, 'Now I lay me down to sleep, I pray the Lord my soul to keep, If I die before I wake, I pray the Lord my soul to take. Amen.' "

Soon, clever as he was, Shaun had learned all the words and could say the entire prayer himself along with his mother. It was very important to Shirley and Jack that their son grow up to be "a Christian gentleman and dedicated citizen," as she once said.

When Shaun was just little more than three years old, he was joined by a new arrival in the Cassidy household. It was another boy for Shirley and Jack, this one named Patrick William, born January 9, 1962. As much as Shaun echoed his mother's looks, so did the new baby, Patrick, remind people of Jack Cassidy.

Shirley spent most of her second pregnancy preparing Shaun for the arrival of another baby explaining very carefully to him, in terms that a three-year-old would understand, how babies were made and how they grew. She answered all his inquisitive questions very carefully and hoped to stimulate his interest in this addition to their family. Of course, she also wanted to assure Shaun that he would still be loved as much as he had been before, that she would love her two children equally.

The idea of his mother having another baby was not an entirely new one to Shaun. One day after visiting a young friend who had just had a baby sister, Shaun returned home and announced to his mother, "I want a baby sister." "Maybe your wish will come true," replied Shirley, who did not know at the time that she was pregnant.

When Shirley discovered that she was indeed expecting another baby, Shaun was thrilled. Whenever he would see a baby, he would say to his mother, "When am I going to get mine?"

For a time, it seemed possible that Shirley would give birth to twins. When Shaun heard that, he solemnly told his maternal grandmother in Pittsburg, "If it's a boy, we'll name him Patrick William; if it's a girl, we'll name her Erin. If there are two babies, I'm going to make one go right back to Mummy's stomach because I don't want two."

Shaun never had to deal with that situation because there was only one baby. He was named, just as Shaun told his grandmother, Patrick William. As soon as Patrick was born, Shirley took care to eliminate any feelings of sibling rivalry on Shaun's part and paid as much attention to Shaun as she could, even with the chores of watching over the new arrival and recuperating from the birth itself. Whenever the baby received a gift, Shirley tried to give Shaun one too. She felt it was important that Shaun feel as loved and as cared for as before.

Shirley's maternal wizardry worked. Shaun was crazy about his new baby brother and fairly doted on him. He loved to hover over the little one, wanted to hand him his bottle, even hold him in his young arms. Shirley allowed Shaun to hold Patrick while she assisted him by holding both of them together. Shaun was so fond of his new brother that he called him, "his baby." Shaun perpetually displayed a strong proprietary interest in his little brother, caring for him as much as he could.

For Shirley and Jack, Patrick was a double measure of happiness. Shirley of course had wanted a girl, but when she saw how much Patrick looked like Jack, she was delighted. After all, Shaun looked so much like her, and now Patrick was the image of his father. The two boys were perfect complements to one another.

In 1964, Shirley had her third child, another son and named him Ryan. Now Shaun had two brothers and an older half-brother.

From the first, Shirley remembers that Shaun was interested in girls. He recalls his first so-called love affair when he was in the first grade, but his mother remembers that it was even earlier than that. On the contrary, she notes, Shaun was aware of the opposite sex when he was just six months old.

"Those three sons of mine have asked and asked and asked me a million questions about girls," she once said. "Not having any sisters around, they are very curious about what makes girls tick . . . why they seem to think the way they do . . . why they do what they do!"

Did Shirley answer the questions to Shaun's satisfaction? All Shaun will say is a hesitant yes and then adds, "But there are some things about girls I'll never understand . . . but that's nice."

When Shaun was four years old, he had a girlfriend named Candy with whom he would play and frolic on top of a wooden horse on the lawn of the Cassidys' Bel-Air home.

One thing that didn't particularly interest Shaun at first was his mother's career as a glamorous and famous movie star. Shirley, still very much the old-fashioned girl from a small town in Pennsylvania, was actually quite glad about this. She didn't want her son to grow up with too many stars in his eyes.

Shaun did visit Shirley on the set of *The Courtship of Eddie's Father,* a movie in which she starred with Glenn Ford in 1963. But he never saw that film on the screen. One of the first movies in which he saw his mother as an actress was *Pepe,* which he went to when he was only about two years old.

When he saw the movie, the inevitable happened. Shaun, like most offspring of actresses and actors, became very confused and bewildered about who the real Shirley Jones was. Was she his mother or the lady on the screen? He didn't know, until his mother carefully explained it to him. That reinforced Shirley's decision to keep Shaun away from her movies until he was older and could understand that she wasn't two people, but was simply playing a role.

When *The Music Man* was first released in 1962, although it was very much a wholesome, family picture, Shirley at first refused to allow Shaun to see it. In that film, she played a librarian who falls in love with a traveling salesman, played by Robert Preston. Despite the fact that many of Shaun's little friends saw the picture, Shirley thought it would confuse him.

"I'm not too keen on him seeing me on the screen, until he's older," Shirley commented, in defense of her position at the time. "I don't like the idea of his seeing it, because thinking of me as a movie star might make me seem different from other mothers. I want him to feel the same way about me as any other child feels about his mother. As it is, kids sometimes say to him, 'Your mom's a movie star.' I wish they wouldn't but of course I can't stop it."

Although there were obviously special privileges that came with being the son of a movie star, Shaun was never spoiled or sullen or ill-tempered. Shirley tried very hard to raise Shaun in a normal manner, given the fact that he was growing up in Hollywood and his parents were both in show business. The result was that Shaun and his two younger brothers grew up never thinking that they were better than anyone else. Maybe they felt luckier, but never better.

Shaun was always an irrepressible kid, the kind who would laugh and tease and giggle a lot. One time, a reporter came to interview Shirley, and Shaun insisted on staying in the room with his mother to help answer questions.

He was always good at play-acting. When he would tell how it was when an elaborate structure that he and a friend had made out of bricks had toppled to the floor, he illustrated the story himself by falling to the floor and tumbling over—and he'd always laugh when he was through.

Even Shirley was amazed at Shaun's good humor and his serene, sweet nature. "Shaun our older boy has always been charming and placid," she once remarked, "but Patrick has a terrible temper. Shaun has always been easy and even tempered and sleeps and eats well. Patrick eats pretty well, but he won't take a nap.

With three, often rambunctious boys, there were often three-way scrapes in the Cassidy household which sorely tried their mother's patience. There are times, naturally, that boys will be boys, and the three Cassidy males would fight and quarrel.

"I can take just so much," Shirley said once, "Then I lose my temper. When I do it's usually because I've been had. If you've ever handled kids then you know they can be pretty conniving little devils at times."

Shaun would be the first to characterize his childhood as one filled with warm, loving, and wonderful memories. Despite the fact that he was a show biz kid, he had a remarkably normal and considerably average upbringing. This is borne out by his recollection of his favorite childhood experience. It's not of meeting a certain star or going to a glittering party; something which one would expect of a kid brought up in Hollywood. Instead, it's a memory that would strike a similar chord with most other teenagers.

"I think," says Shaun with a smile, "it was when I was eleven or twelve and I got a mini-bike for Christmas. I was really surprised, because my parents had spent the whole year telling me I wasn't going to get it. I was happy when I saw it."

Shaun's childhood was one filled with love and brothers and birthday parties; fun holidays, baseball, motorcycle riding with David, listening to music, going to the beach, playing, laughing, sometimes crying, but in may ways, in surprising ways, it was very much your average boy-next-door type of life.

One aspect of Shaun's childhood of which he was definitely not fond, was school. He never really liked going to school all that much and confessed that he hated high school. This might have been due to the fact that before he was finally graduated, Shaun attended no less than three schools. He was shipped away to boarding school in the East, in an attempt on his mother's part to give him time away from the show business environment. That was probably one of the saddest times in Shaun's life—he had just formed a band with his Los Angeles pals, and he felt very alienated being out in the New York area.

"I graduated high school—after attending no less than three schools—and right now, I have no plans for college, though that might change. I started out at Beverly Hills High which was my local high school but I didn't like it at all. . . .

"Beverly Hills High is the trap of all time," he adds.

Both Shirley and Jack didn't exactly think that it was the right environment for Shaun either. There seemed to be influences there which didn't appear to be the best for their eldest son. For one thing, the usually well-behaved Shaun started displaying a strong streak of rebelliousness. Shaun was starting to lead the kind of lifestyle that didn't at all please his mother. He was getting a little too sophisticated for Shirley's tastes.

Shaun was thus transferred out of Beverly Hills High. "My parents then tried a private school called Horizons, also in the Los Angeles area, and sad to say, I didn't do much better there.

"They finally sent me to a private school in Bucks County, Pennsylvania, hoping to take me away from the glamour of show business—so I'd buckle down and get my work done.

"When they sent me away, I thought how horrible it was going to be. I wasn't interested in school, my only thoughts were in show business. Needless to say, I had a miserable time in school, and besides if my folks knew half of the things that were going on there, they would have told me to come home at once. It seemed that every bad guy was enrolled at that school, and because I was from Beverly Hills, it certainly wasn't any easier for me."

Shaun had been sent off to boarding school, "to learn some values," as he once put it, but he was so miserable there, that all he was doing was brooding. Far from buckling down to his studies, he used every opportunity he could to get away to escape from it all. He was probably spending less time on his school work there than he did in Los Angeles. Realizing his unhappiness, Shirley finally decided to have him come back home.

"I finally ended up back at Beverly Hills High and did finish up there," he recalls, adding that his nickname was "Ziggy" in high school. "Not a terrific high school career—but I'm sure glad I got my diploma." He was graduated in June 1976, and comments that "When I finally returned to Beverly Hills High, I had a different perspective on everything. . . .

"Senior year was really touch and go. I even had to go to summer school to make up physical education! I could make up all the other courses while I was on the road, but P.E? I could see myself running around the concert hall or something. . . . Laps over TV? High school wasn't a very enlightening experience but

I'm glad I finished it in case I ever want to go to college.

"I wouldn't want to raise my child in Beverly Hills. It's not a good place. It's too much of a fantasy land. There are no real values. Fortunately, my parents taught me to hang on to my values and all that, but it's still easy to get caught up in it when you're constantly exposed to it."

Although he was frankly discouraged from entering show business as a youth, that didn't stop Shaun from embarking on a sort of amateur career in his own way. He formed his own band in the seventh grade, shortly after he learned to play the guitar. That wasn't his first stab at performing. When he was even younger than that, he used to perform for the kids in the neighborhood, by doing magic tricks at parties, even putting on his own shows.

When he became involved with music, it had already started to take up a good bit of his time; time that his parents felt would be better spent on homework. Shaun was playing with his band at parties and at dances and as the lead singer, would have to rehearse frequently. He even talked about quitting school, much to his father's dismay. His father had never finished high school himself and always wanted his children to get their degrees before they became entertainers. That was very important to Jack Cassidy.

In the midst of homework and other school concerns, however, Shaun was never able to forget the razzle-dazzle world of show business and never forgot his desire to be a performer, even while sequestered away at boarding school in Pennsylvania.

When he was a junior in high school, he was allowed to tour with his mother during the summer months, in a stock production of *On a Clear Day You Can See Forever*. That was in 1975, and Shaun received very complimentary reviews for his singing and acting ability in that show. He played the part of James Preston. He had also had small parts on stage in productions of *The Sound of Music, High Button Shoes* and *Oliver*. Later that year, Shaun starred in his first film *Born of Water* which was released in June 1976 and made for the American Film Institute. He also sang the theme song called "Comin' Home Again" for a television movie which aired in the fall of 1976.

All these chores were really not full-time work, and Shaun longed for the day that he could embark on a show business career without anything in the way. He knew that he could never quit school and that it was simply a matter of time before he had his diploma in hand and was allowed to pursue singing and acting with as much vigor as he wanted. It's no wonder that shortly after Shaun graduated from Beverly Hills High School, his career really took off. It was what Shaun had been waiting for; it seemed, most of his life. He was at last doing what he really wanted to do—singing and acting, and well on the road to becoming the teen idol that he is today.

4

Long before flaxen-haired Shaun Cassidy became a teen idol of the video airways, he was a heartthrob in Europe first and then in America by dint of his singing career. Unlike half brother David Cassidy, who parlayed his small screen stardom into a steppingstone for a musical career, Shaun reversed the process. He ascended the heights of pop music first, then went on to conquer TV viewers. As he readily confesses today, as much as he enjoys and is creatively fulfilled by acting, music is his first love.

"Writing and performing music is my love," he confesses, with an earnest, boyish smile. "And acting is my hobby, although I do like baseball."

It was really through music that Shaun launched his show business career, at the tender age of sixteen, when he released his first single. Acting had been off-limits to him, prohibited by his protective mother who, despite the pleas of her oldest son, did not want him to become a child star. So Shaun, determined to gain an early foothold in show business, even if he couldn't do it by acting, decided to concentrate on music. Considering how musically talented his two parents were—Shirley's career was really launched by her great singing ability—it was a wise choice.

Shaun took up the guitar and the piano when he

was about twelve. Shortly after, when he was in the seventh grade, he formed his own band, called Every Mother's Dream. The band would perform at parties and school functions in the Beverly Hills area. Shaun really loved that.

Later on Shaun formed another band; this one, a quartet called Longfellow. Shaun was lead singer of the group that was very much in the hard rock tradition. In fact, there was just a touch of the punk rock effect in that band back then—Shaun often performed shirtless, with just pants, suspenders, and a bowtie. Most of the members, who included good friends Bobby Graham, John "Bugs" McKenna, and Robby Scharf sported long hair, very much in keeping with their rough sound.

"That was back in 1973 and 1974," reminisces Shaun. "Although we weren't too successful, it was a great learning experience for me. Plus I made some great friends."

Part of the reason the group finally disbanded was because Shaun was sent off to boarding school in Pennsylvania. His mother envisioned Shaun becoming the newest singing sensation, idol of millions and object of so many young girls' ardent desires. Shirley decided that Shaun was too young to be a pop idol and shuttled him off to school in the East. Although Shaun corresponded with the band as much as he could, it was difficult to keep it together when the lead singer was on the other side of the country and one by one, the members dropped out.

The fact that Longfellow was gradually becoming extinct did not deter Shaun from pursuing his dream. Even while he was at school in the East, he composed songs and trekked into New York on the weekends to meet with musicians and play in jam sessions. He just couldn't get music out of his blood.

When Shaun returned to school in California after his fiasco with boarding school, he resumed his singing career. While he was rehearsing and practicing and composing in America, it was in Europe that it all started happening for him. Long before Shaun became a household word in America, he had become a popular and beloved teen star for millions of European teenagers. He had sung in concerts abroad and appeared on European television shows; his winning, innocent face adorning the covers of so many magazines in Germany and other European countries.

Shaun released his very first record, called "Morning Girl," and a single in January 1976. He was only seventeen when the debut 45 rpm was released in Europe. Almost right away, it started vaulting up the charts to the Top 20 hits on the European music scoreboard. That was followed quickly by another fast hit called "That's Rock 'N' Roll" which earned Shaun his first gold record in Australia. That summer, Shaun embarked on a smash tour of Europe; a battery of sell-out performances and where he was met with the same kind of screaming adulation and devotion that had greeted David Cassidy only a few years before. The enthusiastic fans treated Shaun like a conquering hero as they broke through the police lines in Germany. When he left Europe, bound for Australia, the fans swelled around the radio station where Shaun was performing in that Down Under country. They carved their initials and threw their bodies on his limousine when he came back to sing in Detroit.

No wonder Shaun has said, "I know I have the power to whip audiences into a frenzy." He added, with a wisdom older than his years, perhaps absorbing the lessons learned by watching what David went through, "But I never will. It's sick."

In Germany, *Bravo* magazine called Shaun the Singer of the Year. He was also awarded the Otto award for being the biggest new star of the year in Germany. His face often appeared on the cover of *Popfoto*, a Dutch magazine, the English *Fabulous 208*, and *Jackie*. On countless occasions he appeared in European versions of our American Bandstand and other musical shows, called *Tops of the Pops* in England, *Super Disco* in Germany. Long before he became famous with "The Hardy Boys," Shaun was a TV hero in Europe.

Shaun came home after another European tour during the summer of 1976 with the reputation as a major teen idol in Europe. He had already established his credentials in Europe; now it was time for America to discover the talents of young Shaun Cassidy.

When Shaun tried out for "The Hardy Boys," it was really on a lark. His agent had suggested that he get some acting experience under his belt, so he tried out for the part of Joe Hardy.

Actually, the show helped catapult Shaun's musical career into even greater prominence. His first United States release, called "Da Doo Ron Ron," a remake of the Crystals hit of 1963, was sung by Shaun on "The Hardy Boys." It was almost simultaneously released on the Warner Brothers Curb label in spring of 1977, and quickly climbed up the charts to the number one position. The single was so successful that Shaun soon after cut an album; his very first, called simply "Shaun Cassidy," also on the Warner Brothers Curb label.

The album "Shaun Cassidy," released in June 1977, received generally favorable reviews from listeners who appreciated that brand of mellow rock. *Billboard* called it "an interesting blend of music which offers Cassidy a chance to display his diverse vocal ability." Shaun showed a basically simply style on the album, but there is a catchiness to his singing. The LP featured songs from 1961 to the present, including such golden oldies as "Hey There Lonely Girl," "Take Good Care of My Baby," and of course the single "Da Doo Ron Ron." By the end of June, the album had made the charts, and by July of that year both the singles "Da Doo Ron Ron" and "That's Rock and Roll" were riding high across the country.

"Shaun Cassidy" went double platinum before the end of the year, selling over two million copies. Before the year closed, however, Shaun came out with another LP; "Born Late," released in November 1977.

"Born Late" was not named for a song on the album. The title was instead, inspired by Shaun's own feeling that he was . . . well . . . born late. It is further explained on the album notes inside the cover, where, accompanied by baby pictures, there is a dialogue on how Shaun would have much preferred to have grown up years ago. Although he enjoys his life today, he feels that he would have liked to have been born some years before he was. He admits to feeling older than he is, perhaps even old before his time. Shaun will say things like, "I never thought of myself as a teenager."

"Born Late" contains five songs which Shaun wrote himself, such as "Holiday," "It All Escapes Me" and "Movie Dreams." The other five tracks—there were ten in all—included some other oldies and a general potpourri of mellow material that showed how wide his talents were. This album, like the first, was produced by Michael Lloyd who gained a reputation for his work with Donny and Marie Osmond. *Cashbox* magazine said the second album showed "greater confidence and maturity" and predicted that it would have an "overall wide-ranging appeal," not just for the teen set. "Hey Deanie" was the spin-off song which quickly rose to the top of the charts before 1977 ended. That song, as also "That's Rock 'N' Roll," was written by a composer named Eric Carmen.

It's no wonder that Shaun says of 1977, "That was the year it happened for me." Musically he had really arrived in America, a goal he had been building up to with the years of touring in Europe. Three of his songs were hits, a remarkable feat for a newcomer; "Born Late" had sold over a million copies before January dawned. In the space of a few short months, Shaun Cassidy had emerged as one of the leading singers in America; his singles and albums selling in the millions. His debut album, "Shaun Cassidy" ranked seventh in the year's top ten best selling LPs. Clearly, Shaun was a hot shot in the music business.

To celebrate his heady musical success, Shaun was given a $5000 platinum necklace by his manager, Ruth Aarons, for his nineteenth birthday last September—and especially for the fact that his single "Da Doo Ron Ron" had sold so well.

Part of his incredible success, which seemed to have come all in a rush, is due to his distinct musical sound. His producer Lloyd says that "When you hear his records, you know it's Shaun because of his sound, just as you recognize Andy Williams or Elvis Presley. It's nothing a singer can learn; he was that way from the very first."

Critics who put down Shaun's first album as merely a case of bubblegum rock, were surprised to see how far Shaun had stretched his talent and grown musically by the second. A singer who admits to being influenced by such diverse performers as the Beatles, Mick Jagger, Cole Porter, the Beach Boys, and Peter Frampton; he says that he feels true melodic music is the only kind that really lasts and appeals to everyone.

"Every possible chord change has been used so every song you hear is just a combination of lots of other songs put together to sound new. Music is more and more one big melting pot. Very middle of the road. Teenybop music and heavy metal acid rock don't exist anymore. Adults and kids are buying the same records, by Barry Manilow, and Helen Reddy and Eric Carmen. Some like this, some like that. The only new thing is punk rock, which is really trash, just people who don't know how to play."

This statement marks Shaun's own evolution in music. He started out, when he was with Longfellow and even some years after that, with a harsher, more tuneless sound. At that time he was really into hard rock music. Now Shaun has changed to a gentler, softer, more mellow kind of singing, and clearly his audience appreciates that.

Besides the considerable musical legacy inherited from his parents; both extremely capable singers, although neither Shirley nor Jack ever really established themselves as solo performers, Shaun also had some formal training. He studied with the noted Hollywood vocal coach Seth Riggs and majored in music in school. He plays both the piano and the guitar, although he admits that he doesn't play the guitar all that much anymore. When he composes, he likes to peck out a song on the keyboard. "I use the piano for mostly writing songs. I found I could write with more variation using the piano, so I taught myself to play that."

Shaun finds that writing music comes natural to him, almost as natural as breathing. Usually what happens is that two lines, or just a few phrases of music, will pop into his head. What he tries to do from there, is to expand on that germ and make it into a song. That's why he likes to work at the piano, developing the notes into a full-fledged song. Whether he writes the words or the music first depends upon the circumstances. Sometimes he gets an idea that he wants to express in a song and begins to write some lyrics. At other times he works from the music; composing the melody, then adding the words. He recently wrote a song called "Teen Dream," which captures his feelings about being a teenager and learning to cope with freedom and adulthood. He had the idea from a feeling he wanted to express about the teenage years, wrote it into words first and then fit the words to music.

Shaun devotes a lot of energies to his music. He doesn't just dash off a song—sometimes it takes three or four sittings for him to have the kind of finished product that he's pleased with. He wrote a song while he was touring in Australia—it was started on the plane, reworked during his stays at hotels, then polished up in a restaurant.

Ideas and subjects for his songs come from life— what's happening around him, talks between him and his friends, memories he has treasured, feelings he wants to share. He's easily inspired just by the things he hears about and thinks of translating into song.

"I write from the heart," explains Shaun, "about personal experiences, or if I'm very up or down, and have a need to let it out. Every time someone buys one of my records, they're buying an experience of mine, thinking about it for a few seconds. Just the idea of a million people in this country having a song of mine in their living room, it's unbelievable. It's scary to have the power to affect people like that."

Sometimes Shaun has jam sessions with two of his close friends in Hollywood, both of whom grew up with Shaun in Beverly Hills. These two guys are David Jolliffe, who appeared on "Room 222" as a semi-regular, and Bill Mumy, who played on "Lost in Space." He's done a lot of talking and a lot of playing with Bill and David and emerged with some very good ideas and rough songs from it all. Shaun's growing up years in Hollywood were unusual and emotional, not only because of adolescence but because of Hollywood. He shares this experience with both David and Bill.

Shaun's songs are very emotional and full of feeling, much like the way he is himself. Perhaps the reason for his success is because people know that his music is real. Listening to his records is a little like getting to know Shaun better.

Like many creative people, Shaun finds that the idea of a song really makes him feel happy and satisfied. Even if he starts out feeling depressed and wants to convey that feeling in a song; by the time he's finished, he usually finds that the act of creating the song has lifted his depression. Just producing something from his talent makes him feel better.

After Shaun finishes a song, he usually likes to try it out on one or two close friends—to see how they respond to it, to see if it triggers a reaction in them.

Sometimes, he'll just let the song sit for a while, then return to it a few days later to see if he's still pleased with it and that it needs no further improvements.

Despite the knowledge that he works hard on his material, that he tries to do the best he can with songs he has written and with those that he has recorded of other composers, Shaun is still a little taken aback by his sudden and heady success in America.

"I don't know if 'Da Doo Ron Ron' should have been a number one single—I even feel guilty about it sometimes," he says in all seriousness. "I mean, I'm experiencing a level of success that people work years for."

That's why Shaun continues to work hard on his music, to expand his repertoire, to stretch himself as a performer, to try new fields. He wants to convince himself, as well as the public, that this success he's enjoying now is no fluke but a reality that's the result of his ability.

Shaun feels that his success abroad—in Germany and in England—paved the way for his success in America. Moreover, he thinks that it was a wiser career move for him to launch his singing there; where the market is smaller and less competitive, than to just plunge in, in the States, right away. He learned a lot, he says, by going to Europe first, where he could make mistakes and not be swallowed up as a result. It was only after two-years of singing and performing in Europe that Shaun began recording here. By that time, he really knew the ropes and was well prepared for the highly competitive New York and California record markets. He was a highly refined singer, not just an amateur waiting for a break.

Of course, both the show and the record career have

helped each other along. The show helped publicize his singing and his various records released here, and the recording career helped the show gain even more prominence. Interviews with Shaun have always focused on him as a double attraction, sort of a one-man double bill; a singer as well as an actor. Today, Shaun has been dubbed by more than one music publication as the leading prince of teen rock.

This past spring, Shaun completed his first United States concert tour, which began in the beginning of February, in Salt Lake City, Utah, and went through the beginning of April, in St. Louis. All the stops were made on the weekend because of his Hardy Boys schedule. A contract renegotiation called for Shaun to work only three days on the set, so he could have some time off before he embarked on his weekend concert tours.

The response to the tour was nothing short of record-breaking, even astounding, according to rock critics who were used to such surges of popularity of performers. The Hartford Civic Center in Connecticut sold out Shaun's concert on March 4, in less than two hours. Over 2,000 eager fans spent the night in the middle of an extremely cold January in the aftermath of a snow storm, in order to be in line for tickets the next day. It was the fastest sellout, the center reported, in all their history.

Tickets for concerts from Chicago halls to the Nassau Coliseum outside New York City, were selling as fast, or faster, than tickets for the Rolling Stones or the Beatles.

Although he enjoys acting and is content to stay with the series for a while, it's the music that Shaun wants to devote his life to. Television shows can come and go, and the public can grow tired of one idol and fasten themselves to another very quickly. Shaun feels that he'll still be able to have a special place in the entertainment world through his songs—both singing and writing—long after another teen idol will have dethroned him from his unique position.

5

The Story of how Shaun landed the coveted role of Joe Hardy on the TV series "The Hardy Boys" is almost a Cinderella story. It seems to be a case of overnight success for an actor, since Shaun had very little acting experience to his credit. In a way, the story parallels his mother's own fast success, as she was picked as an unknown to play the lead in the movie version of *Oklahoma*.

Shaun had just returned to California from Europe, where he had just completed a smash tour of concerts and TV appearances. He had, as the usually busy Shaun explains, some spare time on his hands. Instead of relaxing and taking it easy, Shaun decided to see what was available in the acting world. Now that he had achieved success as a singer, he wanted to make his mark as an actor.

"I had just finished recording an album and wasn't scheduled to go on tour for another three months," he says. "I didn't really have anything to do, so I started going out on acting interviews. I went out on two and the third one was for 'The Hardy Boys.' "

Not that Shaun was intent on landing a series. He knew from the experiences of his mother and his half-brother David about the strenuous toll of a weekly show and felt committed to his career as a singer and a concert performer. He really considered himself a musician first and an actor second.

As he comments, "I was kind of against doing a series because they take up so much time and I knew I'd have to put my music into second position. But this is really a good series."

There were also practical considerations. His manager suggested, Shaun recalls, that "It might be a good idea for me to get some acting experience if along the long and winding road I'd want to act some more. Then I'd have some experience under my belt."

When Shaun tried out for "The Hardy Boys," he wasn't really aware at first that it was actually a series. He thought it was a one-shot television movie.

As proof of his ability to make it on his own, without using the names of his parents to gain parts, Shaun tried out for the part of Joe Hardy; the producers and directors unaware that he was the son of Shirley Jones and Jack Cassidy. They did know about his concert career, but as far as they were concerned, he was just another fledgling actor.

"They didn't know about my family at the time," recalls Shaun, obviously proud that he could get the part without any string-pulling. "They didn't find out who I was until later." There was absolutely no "preferential treatment" as he calls it.

Just as he did with his music career, Shaun broke into the competitive world of television acting without any help from his famous mother or father, or his half-brother. He earned the role of Joe Hardy—really earned it—completely on his own, and that's the way Shaun wants all the things that come his way to be.

Even after he tried out for the part, Shaun had no idea that he was very high up on their list. He figured that it was just another audition that didn't pan out.

"I had seen a breakdown of "The Hardy Boys" and thought it would be a good idea to try out for the show. I went to an interview and was told that I'd be hearing from them. I figured it was one of those 'don't call, we'll call you' deals so I forgot all about it. Two weeks later I was called back to read and was told they'd call me. They did and I went back to test. A month later they called and said, 'Congratulations, you've got the part,' 'Great,' I said, 'who's playing my brother?' They said they didn't know yet. Finally it boiled down to eight other guys and I had to come in and test with each of them."

Parker was the eighth and last actor that Shaun tested with. He had been summoned out to California for the part of Frank Hardy, Joe's older brother, after producers had seen his affecting performance as the apprentice lifeguard in the movie of the same name, which starred Sam Elliott.

The producers and the directors sensed, after Shaun and Parker read together, what the audience would also sense after just one episode—that the two young actors have a strong rapport with each other. They really seem like they could be two brothers on the series.

Although Shaun had reservations at first about committing himself to a series, for fear that it would hurt his music career, he found that stardom in the television medium helps his image as a singer. And the reverse is also true. That's why Shaun is one of the most popular teen performers around today; he has achieved success in both fields.

"I thought the show might get in the way of the

music but I've found that the two have worked together beautifully," he admits.

"Now I'll be introduced as a television person here and then as a musician. In Europe, where they already know me as a singer, they'll have to get used to me as a television person because the show is going to be sold there.

"Creatively the show doesn't help my music, but it doesn't hurt either. I've thought about putting a piano in my dressing room so I can write songs while I'm waiting around."

That's typical of Shaun, who doesn't want to waste a minute of his time. He's always thinking of ways he can utilize his free moments.

Shaun did have to make one concession to do the series. He had to get his hair cut. That shoulder length hair that he wore was fine for touring as a rock performer in Europe, but it was not right as the all-American junior sleuth Joe Hardy. So Shaun agreed to have his locks shorn and now wears his hair just below his ears.

When "The Hardy Boys" had their debut on January 30, 1977, with an episode called "Secrets of Bronson's Grave," which was one of the scripts *not* based on a story from the books, the show already had built-in appeal. The series is adapted from the juvenile mystery sagas, written over fifty years ago, by Franklin W. Dixon. With the elements of creaking doors, haunted houses, thieves, and spies, "The Hardy Boys," which today include over hundred volumes, are as much a staple of childhood reading and adventure in books as *The Bobbsey Twins* and *Nancy Drew*. ("Nancy Drew" started out as an alternating show with "The Hardy Boys," but now the character is incorporated on "The Hardy Boys" show itself.) These books have captivated adolescent audiences for the past five generations.

The majority of the books were written in the 1920s and 1930s, but in the 1950s the books were rewritten, mostly to update such out-of-synch time elements as running boards and other obviously old-fashioned things.

The show is based on the fundamental outline of the books. Fenton Hardy, a world-famous private detective based in New York City and retired from the police force, has two teen-aged sons named Frank and Joe who have as much a yen for solving mysteries as their father. They can't pass up an exciting and intriguing case. They've even set up a makeshift laboratory in their basement to add to their amateur detection, which often as not, proves to be as good as that of the professionals.

"The Hardy Boys" are not only brothers, but also best friends. They genuinely like each other as people and enjoy cracking a case together. However, just like in the books, the TV series depicts Frank and Joe as two very different people, with two distinct personalities.

Frank, played by Parker, is a man of the moment, a prankish guy who's spontaneous and sometimes even impetuous. He likes rushing into things, especially when he feels the solution is right around the bend. He's always ferreting out clues and mulling over the evidence, sometimes jumping up in the middle of an unrelated conversation to announce "I've got it!"

His younger brother Joe, played by Shaun, is contrastingly painstaking and methodical. He prefers to proceed with caution, considering various alternatives and never doing anything too hastily. He is the perfect balance for Frank's rush-ahead attitude.

As in the original series, the Hardy brothers live with their aunt Gertrude, since their father is a widower. Gertrude is portrayed by Edith Atwater. Ostensibly, Gertrude highly disapproves of her nephews' intrepid crime-solving and dallying with criminals but is secretly proud of their sleuthing ability and gumshoe talents, and she feels much like a mother would towards the boys.

One way in which the show has been updated is with the characterization of Callie Shaw, who serves as gal friday for the Hardy's detective agency. In the book she was depicted as a rather nondescript, good-natured, shapeless woman. As reincarnated by Lisa Eilbacher, who plays the part of Callie, she is a pretty young woman, as much a draw for the audience as are handsome Shaun and Parker. In addition to her good looks, Callie is also a fearless type who frequently takes part in the brothers' adventures and misadventures.

Some other modernistic touches that the series indulges in, are the use of CB radios, motorcycles, and a van. But the lifestyles and the attitudes of the boys remains the same—as pure in heart and as noble as ever. That's part of the source of the mass appeal of the books which has led to over 50 million copies being sold. Certain clean-cut values are constant. "The Hardy Boys" are the kind of old-fashioned heroes that parents want their kids to be familiar with and read about and watch.

The show isn't all heavy gumshoe work and plodding detective chores. There are many light moments, when foiled again by a tricky clue or a wily criminal, the brothers chuckle and collapse into laughter. The series is also relatively free from violence as the nefarious creatures who are guilty of misdeeds are usually killed or meet their demise off the screen for the most part. Guns, a main ingredient of most crime shows, are rarely brandished. The main element of the show is not violence but suspense, lightly blended with humor and fraternal cameraderie.

Ironically, neither Parker nor Shaun as younger boys were all that familiar with the Franklin Dixon books. Yet both say that they've been reading these classics since the show started—doing their acting homework that way.

"To be honest," comments Shaun, "I was a big Tom Swift fan. But I've started to read the Hardy series—there are over 50 of them now—and I'm writing a script from one for the series. It's called The Flickering Torch."

Actually some of the episodes are based on Hardy Boys novels while some are not. It all depends on which books the producers feel lend themselves to adaptation on TV.

While there is an effort to make the show a 70s kind of program, the series is still not all that different from the books.

"The television version doesn't differ all that much from the books. The flavor of the series is pretty much old-fashioned but the concept has been updated enough so that an audience should be able to relate to it," observes Parker, who also admits that the Hardy Boys' books are new to him.

The danger elements are really played down; there is no acute feeling that the boys are really in danger of losing their lives. It's done more with the good-natured and humorous approach of *Butch Cassidy and the Sundance Kid,* than with the cliff-hanging kind of melodrama of a show like "Kojak." The absence of blood and gore violence is important to the show.

"Though our main thrust is on mystery, there is fun to be had, but I draw the distinction between camp and humor," remarks Hardy Boys' producer Glen Larsen. "We're also putting real contemporary humor into the series, not just the camp humor you find in the books."

Just like the gorgeous trio of "Charlie's Angels" who can be in the midst of a manhunt in the swamps and still look like they just stepped out of a beauty parlor, so do the Hardy Boys always look great—Parker with his college boy, Ivy League look and Shaun with that adorable, fresh-scrubbed look.

"We don't sweat. We don't strain. And our hair never gets messed up. Why? Because we're the Hardy Boys," expounds Shaun, laughing at his own inspiring speech.

"With The Hardy Boys," he claims modestly, "I don't really need to act. It all comes naturally to me. I love the show and I love the part and I get along great with Parker Stevenson. I cringe at the thought of working with someone so closely whom I could not get along with. That is why I am so lucky to have someone as great as Parker to work with.

"I knew right from the start that this would be fun for me and I would be a natural for it. All sorts of neat stuff is coming up.

"I think it's getting better and better. The stories are improving and the characters are becoming more like Parker Stevenson and myself. My only concern at this point is that the Hardy Boys are supposed to be about 16; well, I'm 19 and Parker's 25 already, and if we do four or five seasons, we're going to wind up looking like the Over the Hill Gang.''

Despite the fact that many of the mysteries were originally conceived over fifty years ago, Parker feels that there are many contemporary and really timeless aspects about them. That, he feels is why the stories have been popular through so many years, even as times and tastes have changed over the generations.

"The show is contemporary," Shaun agrees, "because we're contemporary. Haunted houses are ageless—they've been written about for hundreds of years —but these stories depend on the characters to give them believability. Parker and I are perfect for our roles, because we can inject the necessary amount of 'now' into the stories, while still being able to carry over the mood of the past. As you watch the series develop, you'll see how a story based in the past can work in the present."

Since Shaun and Parker started working on the show, they have had their share of adventures—some of which were not in the script! They proved to be pretty hair-raising moments for both of them.

During the filming of one episode at midnight at Malibu Beach in California, Shaun was working on a scene where he had to fall into the water. There were all the adequate safety precautions for the tricky shot, including a trained lifeguard standing by, and spotlights ready to shine in case of an accident. Suddenly there was a splash, and Shaun fell into the icy water. But the cameras were not going and no sound was being recorded. It was a mistake—Shawn tripped and fell into the water. It was not part of the script, but an accident.

Fortunately, the lifeguard who was standing by in the event of such a mishap, dives into the water and retrieves a slightly stunned and very cold Shaun Cassidy.

Another time Shaun was scuba diving in a glass-sided tank. Suddenly it looked as though the glass was buckling and beginning to crack.

With a shudder, Shaun recalls the danger he would have been in, if he had not noticed and didn't swim out right away. "If that window had broken, the water pressure would have shoved me right through the broken glass. I could have been cut to pieces!"

During another episode which featured a leopard, there were also scenes which didn't appear on the TV screen. The leopard was supposedly stalking the fictional forest of Witches Hollow, but in real life, he was actually scaring the wits out of Shaun and Parker. The cat at one point escaped from its trainer, and a nervous and anxious pair of Hardy Boys, appearing not quite so intrepid as they do on the air, were cowering in a corner.

"Another thing that I wasn't too thrilled about happened in the second show," recalls Shaun. "They had me hanging off a 500-foot cliff at four o-clock in the morning on a windy, freezing night—just supported by a thin wire harness!

"I was blowing all over the place and just hanging on to this little wire."

Another off-screen spine-tingling event occurred when a car that was supposed to be parked on a hill started sliding down the grade towards Parker. It was another mishap that was not in the script but again part of the routine of doing an adventure series where things like this can happen.

Shaun and Parker have to be particularly careful when they go on location. If it's in the woods or in a jungle, they have to be wary of snakes or other dangerous animals that might appear unannounced in their paths. Or they could be swimming when the undertow gets rough, and that wouldn't be part of the show either. Or the jeep they drive could get a flat tire in the middle of a chase.

But the actors who portray the Hardy Boys have learned to accept these pitfalls as part of the acting business. By now, all these mishaps are pretty much greeted by both of them with a shrug—sometimes with a hearty laugh too. They just try to be careful and realize that things sometimes do happen that aren't planned by anyone on the TV show.

Shaun has a rather optimistic way of looking at all this potential disaster. He feels the adventure part of the show is not only exciting for the plot, but for him as a person, too.

"What's even more exciting for me is that I get to live out my fantasies," he explains. "I get to do things that every young person wants to do. Like ride motorcycles, drive vans with CB radios, fly an airplane, scuba dive—everything. In fact one day, after we finished shooting, Parker and I drove our motorcycles around the Universal Studios lot.

"All I know is that I am having a really great time now. The show is much more interesting than a lawyer or a doctor show where you mostly stand around. I get to do things—fun things. I really don't think I will be tired of "The Hardy Boys" for quite a while."

Nor, would most anyone predict, will audiences get tired of the show—especially when Shaun starts singing. As proof that art can imitate life, in one episode called "The Mystery of the Flying Courier," Joe Hardy launched his singing career at a popular fictional discotheque in the fictional town of Bayport, Massachusetts. It also marked Shaun's debut as an American singer, since previously he had gained fame from his music in Europe.

Dressed casually in a rugby shirt, Joe Hardy, as played by Shaun, entered himself in talent night at the discotheque with a rendition of the 1963 rock hit by the Crystals called "Da Doo Ron Ron." It was also, not coincidentally, the song that Shaun had simultaneously released as a single himself on the Warner Brothers label. The record consequently climbed to reach the number one spot in the charts.

Yet, Shaun who has never had an acting lesson in his life and figures that he probably never will, says that when he sings as Joe Hardy on the show, it's different than when he performs in front of audiences as Shaun Cassidy, the singer, or when he records for his albums. For one thing, he explains, his approach on the show is less sophisticated, as would be fitting a guy like Joe, who has supposedly never performed professionally but just has this raw talent. On the other hand, Shaun, the seasoned professional, has had years of entertaining credits under his belt.

As he explains, "I really try to keep the two careers separate. When I sing on the show, I'm Joe Hardy singing on the show. I'm never Shaun Cassidy singing on the show. What I do in concert is totally different than what I do as Joe Hardy."

Despite the different approaches in singing style,

Shaun believes the show has definitely enhanced his career in America as a singer. The exposure, Shaun feels, of being on a weekly series has helped make him known among so many millions of fans and paved the way for acceptance of his records. Before, there would be people who would have said "Shaun who?" Now the name Shaun is simply enough. He's become one of the more widely-known performers who just needs the first name to be identified.

But there are drawbacks to working on the show, and Shaun feels the toll can be grinding. It's even more taxing than Shaun thought it would be. He was aware of the long hours that his mother and David logged while doing "The Partridge Family," but it was still a shock to him.

"I used to visit my mom and David on The Partridge Family lot, and it's harder work than I thought it would be by just watching it. Long hours. But the times goes quickly. I'd rather be shooting a scene than waiting around between scenes while they change lighting and so on."

And the show can hurt a guy's social life, as Shaun, although pleased with his success, is wont to gripe. "Being that we're shooting from 7 o'clock in the morning until 7 o'clock in the evening, I don't have time to socialize. . . . It wouldn't be fair for me to pin anyone down. My schedule is crazy."

What Shaun did want to pin down, and he's succeeded with each episode of "The Hardy Boys" so far, is the character of Joe Hardy. The directors and producers never really set down in definite terms the type of guy Joe is. It was more or less up to Shaun to figure out, based on reading the Dixon novels and his own native intuition, what kind of person Joe would be.

The same is true of Parker and the character of Frank Hardy. He also had to help shape the personality of Frank Hardy, based on what the writers created and his own acting skill.

"What we find most difficult," remarks Shaun, "is learning just what the characters of Joe and Frank Hardy are. . . . In the beginning of the series, hard and fast rules of characterization are never laid down—so it's difficult for writers and actors to get into character development. . . . The motivation behind the characters is constantly changing."

Unlike others who regularly play a certain character, like John Travolta as Barbarino and Henry Winkler as Fonzie, Shaun feels that there's no real trap in continuing to play Joe Hardy for a few years or as long as the show would run. For one thing, Joe is less of a stylized character than Fonzie and Barbarino, less of a specific type. That's how Shaun feels and that's what he thinks is an advantage to his role. The main trait that Joe has, as he puts it, is that he's "young." He feels that the transition from Hardy Boys to other types of roles would be less difficult than say, switching to other characters from the Fonz.

A typical day for Parker and Shaun on the set begins early—shooting usually starts about eight o'clock in the morning. Bleary-eyed Parker and Shaun arrive, most days, still rubbing sleep from their eyes about an hour before shooting, to be made up and costumed appropriately for the scene. When shooting begins, it doesn't always progress smoothly. Sometimes a certain scene is shot as much as five or six different ways —first with a closeup shot of Parker or a certain angle shot on Shaun, so that later the editors can decide which one looks best. There can be script changes too, if a line doesn't sound right. Or there can be stage directions changes. In one scene where Parker and Shaun emerged from a bank carrying a lot of money, they were instructed to look around fearfully. Shaun, using that native acting ability that he displays so often on the set, protested that that kind of look would be stupid. He thought it would be a dead giveaway to the thieves on the street that the boys were carrying a lot of money. Shaun's suggestions were adhered to, and the stage directions were changed.

There is also what seems to be an endless amount of waiting time for actors on movie and TV sets—lights and equipment to be adjusted for scene changes when directions for those aren't quite right, conferences held about proposed changes, sound to be adjusted, or a special effect improved. There are also constant make-up changes, since under the hotlights, make-up can turn colors and run. During the periods between scenes, Shaun and Parker keep busy. There are business calls to be made, scripts to be studied (especially when changes have just been made), fan mail to be read, interviews to attend, and occasionally the boys take time out to eat. It never becomes boring, but it becomes very frantic and hectic. At the end of the day, sometimes as late as eight o'clock at night, it's only natural that the boys would be utterly bushed. They usually try to revive themselves with a hot shower and a good meal.

Even off the set, "The Hardy Boys" aura, even for Shaun as a singer, is never very far away from them. Both are constantly recognized from their roles on the show—especially when they're together. They particularly like it when fans know them by their real names —not just as Frank or Joe Hardy.

"It really depends," says Shaun. "Sometimes they'll say 'Hey you're one of the Hardy Boys. Other times they'll use our first names. We're both starting to be recognized more now especially when we're out together. But no matter which names people call us, Joe and Frank or Shaun and Parker, it's a great feeling when fans come up and say hello. We both think that's one of the best things about being 'The Hardy Boys.' "

As the episodes progress, Shaun looks forward to developing his acting ability and also to doing more singing on the show. "I have fun doing it and the viewers seem to like it too," he explains. When Shaun first sang, back in 1977, the mail poured in—all of it favorable and wanting more of Shaun hitting the high notes.

Actually, the Sunday night series, which stars Parker and Shaun, is not the first TV rendition of these ageless mystery stories. In the 1950s, "The Hardy Boys" features were a continuing part of the "Mickey Mouse Club" show. The series ran for twenty weeks during 1956 and 1957 and starred Tim Considine and Tommy Kirk as the juvenile sleuths. They were much younger in the roles than Shaun and Parker are. That's one of the ways this new show differs from that program. The producers of today's Hardy Boys felt the "aging" process was necessary so that Frank and Joe could become involved in more different and dangerous situations. Also, the Frank and Joe of the 1950s show used bicycles as their means of transportation, while today's brotherly team use motorcycles and a van—that's one of the differences that gives this series a contemporary look. There's also a different look to the way today's Frank and Joe dress

—more often than not, they're sporting natty suits, sweaters, and sportswear, while yesteryear's Frank and Joe knocked about in jeans and tee-shirts, sometimes flannel workshirts, when jeans were just old clothes to hang around in—not something that could be chic to wear anyplace.

"The Hardy Boys" was also revived in 1967 for television. At that time the show for NBC was a one-shot deal, when actors Rick Gates and Tim Matthieson starred in a one-hour special based on one of the mystery novels.

Today's Frank and Joe are definitely doing their crime-solving in a more sophisticated environment than the Frank and Joe of yesteryear. That was pretty much kiddy fare, as indicated by the fact that the series was showcased on "The Mickey Mouse Club" show. Today's series have enough elements of intrigue, suspense, and mystery to make an exciting show for older folks too, as is indicated by the cross-section of viewers it garners each week. That's why the show could last as Parker and Shaun get older; because more elaborate and complicated plots could be developed for them as they age.

In the meantime, with all the fuss about camera angles, lighting, changed lines, stage directions, and which shot to use, there always seems to be one primary thought at the foremost part of Shaun's and Parker's minds as they film the show.

As Parker put it, after a quick glance through his script, "Hey, Shaun, who gets the girl this week?"

Photo by Bob Deutsch

Shaun Cassidy receiving four Gold records for European sales at La Scala restaurant. *Photo by Audrey Chiu—Michelson Agency*

Above: Here's Shaun back in 1968, with his Mom, Shirley Jones, and brothers Ryan and Patrick. *Photo by Phil Roach— Photoreporters, Inc. Below:* Shaun with his Mom and Dad, Shirley Jones and the late Jack Cassidy. *Photo by Bill Holz—Michelson Agency*

Shaun appreciates his fans. Whenever his busy schedule permits, he reads and answers many of his fan letters. *Photos by Tony Costa—Sygma*

Shaun gave the bride away at his Mom's wedding to
Marty Ingels. *Photo by Nate Cutler—Globe Photos*

Shaun and brothers Ryan and Patrick share a happy moment with their Mom and her new husband Marty Ingels. *Photo by Nate Cutler—Globe Photos*

Photos by Nate Cutler—Globe Photos

Photo by Tony Costa—Sygma

Shaun and Shirley Jones out for the evening at the 1972 Academy Awards. *Photo by Phil Roach—Photoreporters, Inc.*

Shaun with his Mom and brothers Ryan and Patrick in 1971.
Photo by Phil Roach—Photoreporters, Inc.

Shaun and Ryan Cassidy. *Photo by Ralph Dominguez—Globe Photos*

Shaun's Mom, Shirley Jones, received the Genii Award given
by American women in Radio and Television for outstanding
achievement by a woman in that media. *Left to Right:* Jack
Cassidy; Shaun's friend, Shawn Harrison; Shaun Cassidy and
Shirley Jones. *Photo by Frank Edwards —Fotos International*

Back in 1973, Shaun was the lead singer in the hard rock band Longfellow. *Photos by Frank Edwards—Fotos International*

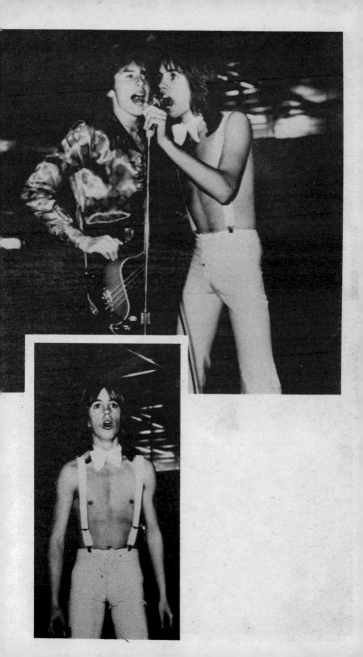

Shaun and a fan at the time of his reception of the Bravo Magazine Award in 1977. *Photoreporters, Inc.*

Shaun certainly is Number 1 among his fans! *Photo by Ralph Dominguez—Globe Photos*

Left to Right: David Jolliffe, Laurie Bartram and Shaun. *Photo by Ralph Dominguez—Globe Photos*

Parker Stevenson and Shaun on location for their hit TV show "The Hardy Boys" *Photo by Audrey Chiu—Michelson Agency*

Photo by Tony Costa—Sygm

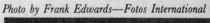
Photo by Frank Edwards—Fotos International

Photo by Tony Costa—Sygma

Above: Shaun joined singer Rick Springfield at a Hollywood party. *Photo by Frank Edwards—Fotos International Right:* Shaun with Charlie's Angel Cheryl Ladd, at the annual "Golden Apple" Awards luncheon in 1977. *Photo by Frank Edwards—Fotos International*

Above: At the annual "Golden Apple" Awards luncheon Shaun met Kevin Brophy of TV's "Lucan" series. *Photo by Frank Edwards—Fotos International*

6

Handsome, clean-cut, and solid-jawed, Parker Stevenson is the other half of the television Hardy Boys team, the 26-year-old actor who plays Frank Hardy on the show.

While Shaun is the product of a solid show business upbringing, with roots very firmly planted in a Hollywood tradition, Parker reflects the East Coast and upper-middle-class environment in which he grew up. Parker could very well be the boy who sat next to you in third grade, and who just happened to become a movie and TV star when he got older.

Parker was born in Philadelphia, Pennsylvania, On June 4, 1952—that makes him a Gemini. Actually his real name is Richard Stevenson Parker, but he couldn't use the name Richard Parker because another actor already had that name registered with the Screen Actors Guild. When he suggested Richard Stevenson, there was an actor with that name also, so Parker, as he's now known in the business, settled on Parker Stevenson, the name which he now prefers.

Parker's father Richard is an investment advisor, and his mother is the former Sarah Meade, who has acted professionally and now does commercials from time to time. "But if you ask her," Parker says, "she'd say that mostly she's a housewife." Yet, obviously that's where Parker inherited his considerable acting ability. His mother's contacts and experience with the business paved the way for Parker's early immersion into acting.

"Growing up with an actress in the family," he recounts, "I couldn't help but see how she reacted to things."

Although Parker's birthplace was Philadelphia, he actually grew up in Westchester, New York, in a town called Warminster. His parents still live there today, in the house where Parker spent most of his youth, along with his younger brother Hutch, who is now fourteen. Parker also has an older sister named Sara, who is married and has a little boy—which makes him an uncle. Even now that Parker has settled in California to work on "The Hardy Boys," he still thinks of himself as a New Yorker.

Parker has always felt a warm and close relationship with his parents, even during those turbulent teen years. He recalls his childhood as a very happy one and says, "I've been lucky having terrific parents. I respect them a great deal and owe an awful lot to them. . . . I've always respected my elders and I think that half of the things I have been lucky to have in life is because of this.

"I've learned a great deal from my folks, and I'm very grateful. When I was told that I got the role of Frank Hardy on the show, my mother was very excited. As excited as dad was, he more or less cooled his emotions. He tends to be very down to earth and because he's that way, we are. Which I feel is good, especially in this business.

It didn't take long for Parker, as a child, to become turned on to the world of show business and the glamour of the acting profession. Not only because of the work his mother did, but also because Manhattan, town of theatres, movies, and concerts, and real hub of the acting profession, was just a train ride away.

When Parker was just five, he accompanied his mother to a filming session, which resulted in two small TV appearances for the youngsters. His serious-minded father thought that was enough of that, and Parker "retired" from the acting business, at least for a time.

He re-embarked on an acting career in commercials when he was fourteen, and enrolled at Brooks Prep School in Massachusetts. Parker was supposed to have a job as a camp counselor for the summer, and when that fell through, his mother suggested he turn to commercials. His first was for Clearasil, and he started using those All-American-boy good looks for advertising Close-up toothpaste, Rye Shaving Cream, J. C. Penney stores, typewriters, cake, candy, even dog food and deodorant.

"My mother was the prime reason I got into show business," he recalls, flashing that earnest grin. "She had been doing loads of commercials. One summer day, I strolled over to the set, met a few agents, and started doing commercials myself.

"I started doing commercials sort of as a summer thing. Then I started seeing agents and making rounds. Little by little, I started doing more and more. I enjoyed it because it gave me something to do. . . . I've never been pushed into the business which I think is great. In fact, my dad plays everything down. If there is one thing he taught my sister, my brother and myself it's that we should play everything down. We should be in control and have a head on our shoulders.

He wants us to know the value of money and never wants us to take anything for granted."

Despite his early success with commercials, Parker did not seriously consider becoming an actor. He was too interested in school, and ever since he was in the sixth grade, wanted to become ar architect. He was even preparing for graduate school after college in order to pursue architecture. As a youngster, he always attended private schools. First, there was Rye Country Day School in Westchester County, New York; then Brooks Private Academy in Boston, where he learned to appreciate the joys of New England living. It was also at Brooks that Parker was on the rowing team, participating with the school crew in the Princess Elizabeth Cup Race at the prestigious Henley Regatta.

Perhaps the milestone of Parker's tenure at Brooks was his movie debut. He was selected to appear in the film version of *A Separate Peace,* a novel by John Knowles about the beautiful and bad aspects of two boys' complex friendship at a private school. The school was supposed to be Exeter during the 1940s, the story told through flashback. Parker played the part of Gene, the shy and unsure boy who almost hero-worships his classmate Finny, audacious, impulsive, strong, and dominating. But Gene's worship of Finny has its dark side that is demonstrated in the climax of the film when he jostles the limb of a tree on which Finny is standing and thus causes him to have a crippling fall. The story is a poignant, moving one, and Parker garnered generally good notices for his premiere role as the adoring friend.

The producer, Robert Goldston, and the director, Larry Peerce, purposefully picked novices for the film version of *A Separate Peace,* because they wanted the true preppie quality in the leading roles. Parker's photo was submitted by an actress with whom he had worked in a commercial. In that both Gene, the character of Separate Peace, and Parker were prep school students, they shared a certain similarity, but Parker felt that the personality in that role was far more introverted and shy than his was in real life.

He remembers how he landed the role, for which he received about $15,000 for about 10 weeks of work in 1971.

"There were three screen tests and a lot of interviews. They took me to lunch in some fine eating places and I'd order steak. I had lots of steak because there were nine interviews. I have a healthy appetite. It's even healthier when someone else is paying for it. . . . They finally called to say they were interested. A week later they told me I had made it. But I didn't know the part I'd played until the day before we began shooting."

It was then that Parker started toying with the idea of acting as a career. "My architecture ambition kind of faded after that, but I haven't given up on it totally," he says.

After Brooks, Parker enrolled at Princeton, where he was set to major in architecture. However, in 1974, his academic career was again held in abeyance as he landed the role of another preppie in a funny-sad melodrama called *Our Time*. Parker played Michael, in love with a girl at a nearby boarding school called Penfield. The sweetheart was played by Pamela Sue Martin, who would later be teamed with Parker on the "Nancy Drew" series which alternated with "The Hardy Boys." "We've been friends for a long time and it's great that we're both working on similar series at

Universal and have time to see each other," he notes about Pamela, and adds, "there's no romance involved."

Our Time was set in the 1950s, and Parker was a prep school student at a place called St. Andrews. Betsy Slade and George O'Hanlon Jr. were also starred in the story of two teenage girls, and the triumphs and traumas they had with their boyfriends, savoring the joys and sharing the heartaches of their first affairs.

Commented Parker about *Our Time*, "The character in that movie is closer to the way I actually am," referring also to the role he played in *A Separate Peace*. "Being in the movies hasn't made as much of a change in my life as I was afraid it might."

Parker had to curtail his studies at Princeton to make the movie and consequently fell behind a year, since the dean would not allow him to make up the semester. When he returned to college again in the fall of 1973, he resumed his study of architecture and singing with the Princeton Tigertones and rowing on the crew team.

Although Parker had gained by now estimable acting experience, he was still unsure that he wanted to become an actor. He never actually studied acting and only appeared in a few school productions like *Charley's Aunt* while at Brooks. It was important to Parker and to his father that he have a college degree, especially from Princeton, which as a member of the Ivy League complex, is one of the most distinguished colleges in America.

The fact that Parker was able to maintain a levelheaded attitude is due to his father's sensible advice.

"My dad made sure that I kept my head on my shoulders and was always in control. He didn't want me to take anything for granted. . . . I've always enjoyed school."

"I wanted to go to college and study architecture. I was working in New York doing commercials while I was going to school at Princeton, so I just wanted to take courses that would be sort of away from show business. I've always been interested in architecture. . . . I think if I was really a nut about show business, it wouldn't be all happening for me the way it is."

Actually, Parker's well-schooled background and his Ivy League degree—he graduated from Princeton with majors in both art and architecture—give him options that many actors do not have. If he should ever decide to leave show business and give up acting, he could certainly make his living that way.

Or, he says, obviously having considered the matter, "I would go to business school." He would follow in the footsteps of his father and go into the world of business. He had applied to business school, as a matter of fact, in 1976, the same year that Hardy Boys started shooting. His original plan, if the show hadn't been picked up as a regular series, was to attend New York University business school.

Parker, who was always interested in, and always enjoyed school, says, "I think getting the series pushed me into the business more than I expected it to. I've always enjoyed it, it was fun getting my feet wet, but I didn't think I wanted to have a definite career with it."

"I still have tentative plans of taking some courses sometime, but as long as the show runs, I'll be devoting most of my energies to that."

It was while Parker was still a student at Princeton that the proverbial big break in show business came— the turning point that was to make the monguls behind the scenes sit up and take notice of this young talent. It was a break that would lead to Parker's landing the role of Frank Hardy.

Parker was selected to appear in a third movie, an earnest drama about an aging lifeguard. It was called, appropriately, *Lifeguard* and starred Sam Elliott in the title role. Parker played the summer assistant who was apprenticing between college semesters. The film, which was appealing, as well as fun, was a big hit with audiences since its release in the summer. It made Parker, who looked all tanned and muscular in the part, much more of a recognized actor. For the first time, people really knew who Parker Stevenson was, and fans appreciated, not only the way he looked in a bathing suit, but also how well he acted.

But the filming of *Lifeguard* did pose some problems for the real-life college student. He explains, "They had to fly me back and forth between school and the beach where we were filming. I liked the attention but it was kind of rough on me after a while."

Despite the commuting hardships, the role led to bigger and better things for Parker.

"After *Lifeguard,* I got a few television roles—on shows like "Gunsmoke" and "Streets of San Francisco"—but not much else. Then one day I got a call from the Hardy Boys producers. They had seen me in *Lifeguard* and wanted to know if I was interested in testing for the show. I was on the next plane for Los Angeles," he adds, admitting that he was ready to pull out all the stops for a chance like that.

Ironically, although Parker was familiar with the famous mystery series for young adults that featured the adventures of two sleuthing brothers that in turn prompted the birth of the TV show, he was never an avid reader of the books themselves as a youngster. However, he immersed himself enough in the role that by the time the camera was ready to roll, Parker knew all about Frank Hardy.

Talking about his role, which again is in the clean-cut, All-American-boy mold which characterized his previous parts, Parker says, "I wouldn't have taken on the part if I didn't think it was right for me. . . . Obviously there are certain occasions when I think to myself that I wouldn't go along exactly with what's happening—but I'm in the lucky position of being able to do slight rewriting with the script to make it more adaptable to me. I don't change the whole story-line, but if there's a word or a line that I don't like, then I'm at liberty to do something about it.

"There is a lot of interacting between the audience and us with the Hardy Boys, as well as tension and suspense. It is really hard to turn away from an episode of the Hardy Boys once you start watching it."

The thing that athletically-inclined Parker finds especially exciting about filming the series is the opportunity to do his own stunts. For someone as sports-minded as Parker, it's a challenge and a thrill.

"Shaun and I do most of our stunts. They let us do as much as possible."

Sometimes the stunts are just natural extensions of Parker's hobbies, like his and Shaun's scuba diving for treasures underwater. But the episode in which he had to wrestle with a panther was a very new experience for him—as it would be for most people!

In the Hawaii-based Hardy Boys episode, Parker says, "I did some of my own surfing. I did not know how to surf and I went out with my stunt double and learned. Some of the more difficult surfing stunts were taken from footage of surfing championships held in December. That was definitely not me in those really gigantic waves. It's a lots of fun doing stunts for the show, though. They've had us up flying, scuba diving, and lot of fun things.

"The time goes incredibly quickly," comments Parker about the fast tempo of a weekly series. "Often you just get one take. I don't really prefer it that way; I'd rather have more time, but with a series like ours, you can't take that time. The hours are different than I thought they'd be—18 hours a day is something I didn't really expect.

"I didn't realize how long we would sometimes have to work. We've gone for twenty-four hours working several times. It gets pretty grueling, but I enjoy it though. Having something you can be that committed to is nice. I go to sleep with a sense of accomplishment after working those long hours and my days are pretty planned out for me now.

"Some of the filming is done at night to add a note of mystery to the show. We try to do things at night to make it more mysterious—which means Shaun and I are out there running around at night. Working nights is crazy!

"There is a lot of clowning on the set, but not as much as you might expect. There is always pressure to move on and get the next shots. . . . They change the scripts quite a bit. That's partly what takes extra time —learning new lines after they hand us a new script!"

As far as the character of Frank Hardy goes, Parker

confesses that there are similarities between his real personality and his on-camera alter ego. "As the show has gone on, I have found myself putting more and more of myself into Frank Hardy."

Obviously, Parker is enthusiastic about the series which propelled him to superstardom, in spite of the long, grueling hours and the frantic pace, which can leave a guy with little leisure time. Except for one thing, it doesn't faze Parker. That's being away from home, or what he considers home which is New York.

"I suppose the only drawback is being away from my family," he admits. "You see, we're very close and even though I speak to them a lot on the phone, it's just not the same being three thousand miles away. Apart from that, there's nothing about "The Hardy Boys" that I don't like—nothing at all."

Since the series started, especially now that the show has entered its second season, Parker finds himself making a heady salary for someone who's so young—several thousand dollars a week; but with the typical level-headed sensibility that he got from his father, he has not become a spendthrift nor let his lofty income go to his head.

"I'm not spending much of it," he relates soberly. "Mainly because I just haven't got the time to spend it. Anyway, I really have to consider my future and as an actor you never really know what's going to happen, so I think it's sensible to keep most of it in savings for a rainy day.

"I have taken some trips—one to San Francisco and one to San Diego," says Parker, who loves to travel. He's been all over Europe, to Hawaii, New England, and Bermuda. "That's an indulgence for me. I'd been to San Francisco before because I did a "Streets of San

Francisco" guest spot. It was my first time in San Diego and I really enjoyed it. I went one Saturday late afternoon and came back Sunday evening, so I only had one day there—and I spent six hours at Sea World. I love places like that."

Parker can do without the ostentatious trappings of stardom. He likes nice, well-tailored clothes, but nothing extreme or expensive. He has a 1971 BMW that he wouldn't part with for the world, no matter what kind of fancy sports car or coupe were offered him. His apartment is cozy, but hardly intimidatingly affluent or a movie star's palace. It wouldn't be what Parker would call home.

After graduating from Princeton, Parker rented an apartment in New York City, with a college roommate and two other friends, none of them actors. Because of his great love of New York, he's still kept the apartment as a base for his trips back East; but confirmed in his commitment to "The Hardy Boys" and to California, has an apartment there.

"I've moved into a new apartment in West Hollywood," he says," and already fans have started to find out about it. I think they follow me home from the studios at night. It's just a one-bedroom place—very modest but it'll do for the time being. I might consider buying a house here in Los Angeles."

Living in Los Angeles has been quite an adjustment for Parker; one that has its good points and its bad points. For the guy who has so much affection for New York, who loves walking around the streets of Manhattan, browsing and watching the people, it was difficult to become accustomed to the more relaxed and easy-going California lifestyle. It's much more carefree and less hectic than New York.

Then there's the system of the Los Angeles free-ways. As someone who spent his commuting time on the subways and buses and occasionally cabs, he finds the freeway-maze mind-blowing! So much traffic, so many cars, all going at frantic paces and all stuck in traffic jams, with the endless number of overpasses and underpasses. Parker has always loved to walk—"I'm a walker" he boasts proudly—and no one walks anywhere in Los Angeles. Everyone drives.

But Parker is an enthusiastic outdoors type, and the California weather—sunny, warm, balmy,—is a joy, especially since he's so involved with sports like jogging, racquet tennis, squash.

During the past year, Parker has tried to make the transition from being New York oriented to becoming a member of the Los Angeles crowd. That has not only involved accepting the different lifestyle on the West Coast, but also making new friends there.

"Most of my friends are from the East Coast," he explains, adding that many of them are not in show business, but rather doctors, lawyers, bankers, professionals. "I've found that a lot of them have made the trip out here to see me, so I haven't been too lonely. I have made a few good friends in Los Angeles, too," he confesses, explaining that most of his California acquaintances are involved one way or another with show business.

Then too, Parker makes a point of returning to New York, to visit and chat with friends and family, as often as he can. That's not very often, considering his hectic pace on the series, but he has a wonderful time each trip back East.

"I like the excitement back there," he says, his eyes lighting up with sparks. "Every time I get to go to New

York City, I get sort of recharged. There is so much to do there, so much happening. Whether it be a concert or a party or a play or whatever."

One of the good friends Parker made in California is his costar, Shaun Cassidy. Although there's a difference of six years between them, Parker finds that Shaun is mature beyond his years, and that it's a genuine pleasure to be working with him. No, he insists, there's no jealousy or competition between them, despite the fact that Shaun's a better known personality than Parker is.

"I met Shaun through the show and I am friends with him off-screen. Usually when you spend 18 hours a day working with someone, you just want to go home and sleep and forget about them for the rest of the day. But we've gotten to be pretty good friends. We go out to dinner and hang out together, even when we're not working, and I think it helps our roles that we really like each other in real life.

"I know people expect me to say Shaun and I really get along, but it's really true. We really like each other. And we enjoy doing things like going to movies together. We also confer about scripts. We socialize a lot."

That wasn't always the way it was. In the beginning, before the series started, Parker and Shaun had initially decided that it might be best to avoid social contact, to prevent anything happening on the show.

"We had a long talk while we were filming the first show and decided that it wouldn't be a good idea to mix socially for the simple reason that we see each other so much during the day—and sometimes into the night, while we're filming. We both felt that a break would be a good idea."

As the series progressed, and as Parker and Shaun got to know each other better and realized the terrific aspects of one another's personality, that original decision was forgotten and a deep and close friendship was formed. "Shaun's very friendly and outgoing, very funny, very quick, and there are a lot of similarities between Shaun and Joe Hardy," enthuses Parker.

Besides the obvious age gap and background difference, there are differences between Parker and Shaun. "We've got different friends and both of us enjoy doing different things and going to different places.

"What I would really like to say is that Shaun and I have never had one argument! And that's really something considering how temperamental actors are supposed to be. We often eat together at the studio and we talk about our personal lives and sometimes I'll pop around to Shaun's house and other times he'll come to my apartment if he's going by—just to say Hi! I think we've got the ideal relationship."

Since appearing on "The Hardy Boys," Parker gained hordes of fans, the majority of them female. He receives some 1000 fan letters a week, positively sacks of mail. But one of his biggest fans is his younger brother Hutch—whose real name incidentally is Joseph Hutchings Stevenson, hence the nickname Hutch. Parker claims his brother was called Hutch long before the popular series "Starsky and Hutch" debuted on TV. Following in the footsteps of his older brother, Hutch has shown an interest in doing some commercials. Just like Parker and their mother.

"He does look like me," describes Parker, with a large dose of brotherly pride. "We are pretty close, but I'm away so much that it's hard. I'm not home as much as I'd like to be. If I'm not in Los Angeles working on the show, I'm usually traveling. So I don't spend as much time with him as I'd like to. But when I am home we spend a lot of time together.

"He enjoys watching the show. I've watched two of the shows with him. We sit with the family and all watch it together. His friends enjoy the show and he gives me their reactions about what they like and what they don't like. He's been very helpful, actually.

"He was out here on a short vacation and he had a great time. He's only thirteen, so I should imagine he had lots to tell his friend when he went back to school. I loved having him here."

The affection he has toward his brother says a lot about the kind of person Parker is. He's warm, good-hearted, sensitive, kind, and a trifle reserved. Although friendly and caring, Parker is hardly the boisterous life-of-the-party type.

"I think that perhaps in certain circumstances I might come off a bit shy," he admits, "because until I get to know someone really well I just like to listen to what they have to say and feel the person out, if you know what I mean. I don't know if that's what you would call being shy—but if it is, well, I guess I am."

He considers himself a fairly easy-going, take-life-as-it-comes sort of guy, not one of those anxiety-ridden actors. He can shrug off misfortunes and problems fairly easily and has an essentially optimistic nature.

"For me to get angry it takes a lot. Then when I do, I tend to brood about it a lot. I sit on things, I guess."

One of Parker's least favorite times is early in the morning, when, he reveals, he's not a very pleasant person to be around. He's one of those who need a few hours to feel human, not the kind who bound right out of bed in the morning with a ready smile and small talk.

"I'm very grumpy in the morning. . . . I need coffee and a long shower before I can get myself together. I'm not really myself until about 11 in the morning."

Once Parker gets going and emerges out of that early morning funk, he's ready for anything—especially good times and fun. He likes to laugh and to enjoy himself.

"A good joke makes me laugh . . . sometimes I laugh at myself. I laugh at myself quite often actually! I very rarely cry . . . sometimes I get upset at a good movie though."

Nothing really rumples Parker's feathers—it takes something extraordinary to make him frightened. "I don't think I have any phobias or fears or anything like that. I guess I'm not scared. I don't think I even worry too much about anything."

Physically, Parker can well qualify for the idea matinee idol category. He has the classic, All-American, boy-next-door looks, well-chiseled features and fabulous coloring—just the kind of guy that a girl would love to bring home to daddy and introduce as that special man. There's a solid, down-to-earth, sensible air about Parker—he's obviously the kind of guy you can really depend on. You can sense that he has a strong forthrightness and sincerity. He exudes self-confidence, but not brashness, and a feeling of inner security and trustworthiness.

Parker has thick, light brown hair, that he prefers to wear on the longish side—but not too long. It always looks neat and well-combed, no matter what kind of hair-raising escapade Frank Hardy has been through on the show. He's well-built, with a lean, muscular body and weights in at 155 pounds and is an even six feet tall. Parker's eyes are dark blue that have sparkly flecks in them when he laughs or smiles.

What's his best trait? Well, he thinks it's that he really "likes people a lot." When he says that, emphasizing the word "likes," you know it's a sincere evaluation.

As far as activities outside the show go, well, there's hardly a spare minute for Parker to indulge in hobbies, but he's acquired a slew of them. There is a whole gamut of things he enjoys. One of them is photography. Parker says that taking pictures and developing them is his number one hobby.

"I have a 10-year-old Nikon (one of the best-made cameras money can buy) and I love taking pictures. My specialty is scenes—compositions—rather than portraits of people."

The majority of Parker's photos are city scenes, taken in New York, all over town, at various times of the day. They are actually quite good, so good that some of his friends have suggested that he have his own one-man exhibition.

He also winds down from the grind of doing the series by reading, sailing, tennis, and watching television. His favorite show is about another detective—this one the rumpled, always raincoat-clad Lieutenant "Columbo" of the series of that name.

Like most guys his age, Parker loves music and has his own specific tastes. He prefers the songs of the Eagles, Linda Ronstadt, James Taylor, Elton John, but, he adds, "The only group that I can listen to with any regularity is the Beatles. . . . But I listen to some kind of music all the the time. There are certain classical and jazz pieces that I like too. And I love to dance, but I haven't had much of a chance to get out and do much dancing lately."

Now that Parker's in Los Angeles where the only

means of getting about is by car, he enjoys tooling around in his 1971 BMW. He could also get around on horseback if he had to, since horseback riding is one of his favorite pastimes. He's taken a few polo lessons along the way, just enough to make him feel confident on the playing field. He also tried to jog daily but acknowledges that "I have to keep making myself get out. I'd be just as happy sitting at home, relaxing and watching TV."

There's also a bit of the daredevil element in Parker (despite that down-to-earth demeanor) who confesses that if he could do anything he'd love to be able to fly —naturally, like birds do.

"I used to have dreams about being able to fly, and I've even taken soaring lessons—which is about as close as you can get to really flying."

The soaring lessons which Parker has embarked on have also made him skilled at hang gliding, which is about the most dangerous and precarious sport around—showing that Parker has his fair share of bravery and gutsiness.

What else should you know about Parker? Well, his favorite colors are blue and brown, the ones that seem to go best with his hair and his coloring. If you were to fix his favorite meal, you'd prepare a thick steak, and potatoes, since he's a man with that kind of appetite. Parker also expresses a liking for chocolate chip ice cream ("I'm a freak" he says) and Oreo cookies. Yet if you poked around in his refrigerator, all you'd probably find is a little milk, some cereal, and a few pickles!

A considerate, thoughtful person, Parker feels genuine regret that he cannot answer personally all the fan mail he receives, but he declares that he reads as much of it as he can between shows and rehearsals. He says, "I answer some of it. There's a lot of it coming in for the show . . . and it's interesting to get people's reactions. The best place for people to reach us is to write us in care of the show."

The former Ivy Leaguer really appreciates his fans. He loves meeting people and doesn't mind if a total stranger comes up to greet him, as long as it doesn't become a mob scene. "I love to meet my fans," he says and at this point claims that no fan has ever turned him off.

"One girl asked me to sign her arm. I thought that was pretty strange, but I did it because I could tell that she really wanted me to. I think that's the weirdest thing that I've ever been asked to do."

He doesn't mind being recognized as the Parker Stevenson, star of the popular "Hardy Boys" series, although he's very unassuming and matter of fact about it all. He's still the same modest, down to earth kind of guy he was before all this happened. When asked how he feels about being a star, Parker will invariably say, "Is that what I am?"

"That's one of the best things about being in the business," he observes, about being recognized. "I really like it when people come up and say, 'Hey, aren't you. . . .'"

"I enjoy talking face to face with my fans. I like to get to know people."

From all the letters, all the encounters in the street, all the interviews, Parker says that the one question that he gets asked most frequently is, "How did you get into show business?" Most fans realize that Parker isn't from the kind of Hollywood family that Shaun is, and are curious to learn how he got so far so quickly.

Parker is eager to dispense advice about aspiring performers, although he's careful to paint a realistic picture of the odds involved and how trying and arduous an actor's life can be—even when he is successful.

"It's very difficult. It can be very discouraging. There are long periods of time when you're not working. If you're really serious about acting, it takes a big commitment. You have to be willing to wait and really work hard to get anywhere."

Those superstars in show business that Parker himself admires and looks up to are Paul Newman (he idolized the screen king when he was growing up and still does), Marlon Brando, Dustin Hoffman, Faye Dunaway, Jacqueline Bisset, and Colleen Dewhurst.

He is also a big fan of old comedy like the slapstick routines of "The Three Stooges" and the "Laurel and Hardy" TV series.

"I love to laugh," he says, breaking into a big grin that shows off his dimples. "I am always cracking up with Shaun, both on and off camera. . . . Being with good friends and have a cozy dinner—or watching people in general just being happy makes me happy."

And what makes Parker sad? Besides a poignant, tear-jerking movie that can give him a lump in the throat, he gets upset by "getting a flat tire when I'm in a hurry, or being told a lie by someone I trusted."

Honesty is a most important character trait to Parker, and if there's one thing that he seeks in a close friend, it's sincerity.

What about girls? Parker is most certainly one of the most eligible bachelors in Hollywood and very enthusiastic about girls. The demands of the series are taxing, but Parker always finds time to date.

"I like all girls but one with a good personality really turns me on. I don't like a girl who is always down. I guess that's because I enjoy laughing a lot.

"I like a girl with a certain amount of intelligence—one who has a lot of interests and keeps me interested. It's really difficult to explain, because it's a combination of things and the way they come together. I like big eyes and long hair. What I don't like is girls who depend completely on me—I have friends whose girlfriends are like that but I wouldn't want that.

"I notice a certain spark. I like a girl with common sense."

"It wouldn't matter to me if a girl is in show business as long as I can relate to her."

Parker has no special girlfriend now but asserts that he has both played the field and gone steady in the course of his dating experiences. "It's nice to have someone that you're seeing regularly and that you can get close to. It becomes a matter of how much you want to be involved." He also says he would certainly date a fan.

As far as his preferences for what to do on a date, at the top of the list is "Going out for a nice dinner. Just dinner is nice. I like going to see plays, museums, films, shows—doing anything that's new, including eating at a new restaurant. That's what I love about New York City—something's always happening."

Something is always happening when Parker takes out a girl. He's always planned something exciting and fun to do; not being the type of escort who would want to just sit around and hang out. His enthusiasm and his zest for exploring new things is infectious and always makes for a terrific time.

Like most young men, Parker has thought at great

length about marriage and considered the institution carefully, both in sober and earnest talks with his friends, and simply by himself. One of the primary decisions he's made is that now is not the right time to get married, no matter how much he loved a girl, because the demands of his career and his desire to grow and develop further as an actor before he settles down.

"At this point in my life, I want to devote myself full time to my career. I don't think it would be fair to myself or to anyone I might be interested in settling down with now. I don't think you should marry until you are ready to make that kind of commitment."

Parker does feel, though, that someday he will make that commitment, inspired by the success and love found in his own parents' marriage. "If I was guaranteed a marriage like my parents had, I would love, it," he says. Besides, he feels that's the best way for a man and woman to live together.

"I do think I'll get married," he promises. "There's not much time for romance in my life right now, but I know that someday I'll find the right girl and settle down to a married life and probably be a father. It's just right now that kind of life is so far off in the future that I can't even give proper thought to it."

When Parker does get married, he would be very much in favor of having his wife maintain her own career, whether that would be in the acting or another field. A guy who finds himself pretty much in sympathy with the goals and demands of the women's liberation movement, Parker would want the woman he marries to be her own person and have her own life apart and away from their married life together. When Parker finds this unique and special lady, chances that a decision to settle down to a married life may come about, even before he realizes it.

Right now though, Parker is concentrating on acting and looking forward to his professional future, as opposed to a personal one. He'd like to guest star on other series, in addition to his work on "The Hardy Boys." For instance, he'd like to work on "Baretta," perhaps work with James Garner, whom he admires very much.

"I'd like to play a bad guy," he says. That would be a real acting challenge for someone as All-American as Parker is. "I think I could make a good bad guy. . . . I would like to do some things that would be a change from Frank Hardy. I think it is important not to be stereotyped. I would like to do some comedy things too."

Parker has already thought of the possibility of returning to school if things don't work out the way he wants them to in show business. He doesn't seriously think that will happen, but a guy like Parker is always prepared.

7

Shaun Cassidy has a dilemma. Here he is, enjoying the unique status of superstar and teen idol, the veritable heartthrob of millions of teenage—as well as older—girls who would do practically anything to meet him. His boyish good looks have made him the most popular cover personality since Farrah Fawcett. He is to today's generation what Frank Sinatra and Elvis Presley were to theirs. Girls swoon, sigh, and carry on, just for a glimpse of Shaun, just for one fleeting touch of his clothes.

It would seem that Shaun could have any girl he would want in the entire world and yet he can't. The fact is that he is so busy with his duties to the series, his music career, all the chores of his multi-faceted life, that his social life is practically nil. One of the world's most desirable young men confesses that he hardly dates at all.

"I've heard that I'm a flirt, a heartbreaker, a guy that dates a different girl every night, and I have to laugh about it all."

"The truth of the matter is that I'm so busy that it's unreal. It wouldn't be fair for me to ask one special girl to be faithful to me. My schedule is such that I don't have a minute to myself. I'm either off to London or touring around the country. I think it would be terrific to have one special girl, because basically that's the kind of guy I am, but there's just no way. That's why I say 'I can't be true to one girl.' "

On another occasion, Shaun said, "My social life is shot. I tend to date girls that I've known for a while. I went steady for a time, but I had to break it off because the situation was unfair to the girl. Between the series and the concert tours, I'd be gone five months without even being able to see her."

The girl in question, with whom Shaun was dating, was a former classmate of his at Beverly Hills High School, Laura Fox. She and Shaun are still friends; they just don't go steady anymore.

Putting his estimate of his current social life in an even more blunt fashion, Shaun says emphatically, "My romantic life has gone down the drain."

Thus the dating woes of one of television's most popular new stars and an up and coming idol. "I'm so busy I hardly have time for anything anymore, let alone a steady girl," he laments.

Not that Shaun's complaining. He realizes that this sudden surge in popularity, while nothing short of mind-blowing, is also transient and that it could evaporate tomorrow. He knows that there is plenty of time for romance and love and marriage, but stardom is something which is so precarious that you must accept it and live with and enjoy it when it happens—which, as most performers know, is all too infrequent.

Shaun has given very serious thought to what his taste is in the opposite sex and has certain definite requirements for someone he'd want to get seriously involved with.

"I guess everyone has some idea of a dream girl or

guy," he muses, his eyes misty with concentration. "So here's mine: she's warm, open, honest and likes me a lot. She wears little or no make-up and I feel I can tell her everything. I can trust her, that's the most important thing.

"I guess I'm really not too much different from the next guy in that I like girls who are really open and warm. I turn away from girls who are affected, who pile on the make-up.

"What turns me on is a girl who takes care of her body, doesn't wear a lot of make-up and has a brain. Women who are independent thinkers attract me strongly. But I can't take anybody who doesn't know how to be themselves."

As far as particular looks go, Shaun says, "I don't care what color a girl's hair is, whether it's long or short—as long as it looks nice on her. Of course, I would like a girl to dress in whatever's appropriate for the occasion."

Pondering further the question of his ideal girl, Shaun offers, "I tend to give different answers all the time." That's mainly because as a person Shaun Cassidy is changing all the time. "At the moment I can dream only of my ideal girl and because I can't see her, all I can tell you is that she will be romantic—that's for sure! I don't care if she's even an old-fashioned type of romantic."

Shaun initiated his dating life earlier than most guys do—it was partially because of his own precociousness and also the sophistication of his Hollywood surroundings where peer pressure is strong and parents tend to be more liberal-minded and progressive. In any case, Shaun has been dating, double- or single-dating, for about seven years, so he's been able to formulate some thoughts about the relationships he's had and male-female relationships in general. When he talks about dating, it's with a lot more wisdom and seriousness than most young men of his age demonstrate.

"I think feelings are important and all I ever do in a relationship or rather when a relationship is over, is not to try to hurt the other person's feelings. Sadly, it can be difficult at times, but remember, it's me who gets my feelings hurt! When you think about it, there's no real way that you can break off a relationship with someone who wants to continue it and not hurt their feelings. I suppose there are so many ways you can do it but what it all boils down to is all those ways mean the same thing—goodbye."

"The thing I try never to do in a relationship is lie —not even white lies. There was a time when I used to tell white lies, just for the girl's sake, so that perhaps I would relieve her of some of the hurt. But now I find the only way a romance can work is if it is based totally on truth—two people being very honest with each other."

Shaun demands the same sort of honesty from the girls he dates. "Give me a girl who is sincere and honest. I don't like one who is a phony."

His vulnerability and his quality to reach out and touch people add to Shaun's very affectionate personality. He's very demonstrative and prone to display his warm feelings freely. He's not reserved or uptight about showing a girl that he cares.

"I do like a girl who's affectionate, since I'm very affectionate and my dates get mad! But I'm just that way!"

Shaun is the kind of guy who is a snuggler and a cuddler, the kind who would cozy up with a date while watching TV or a movie. He loves to hold hands and squeeze his date's arm or neck. He's often spontaneous and impulsive with his little signs of affection— like suddenly putting his arm around a date at a party and drawing her close. He acts upon his feelings and is very romantic. Occasionally, he knows, it might embarrass the girl he is with, but he figures that the kind of girl who would be right for him would understand and want him to be that way. "If I feel like kissing someone or putting my arms around them, I do it," he declares.

There are, however, few moments for Shaun to be affectionate with that special someone, since he is so consumed by his work in show business.

"I've said it before and I'll say it again. . . . I'm working so hard my social life has gone right down the drain. There just isn't that much time to date—or even to go anywhere to meet girls. It's sad, but that's the penalty I'm paying now for my life in show biz. . . . I usually date old friends who understand what happens when I go out in public. Last summer I just decided to stay home. . . . I do understand it and I realize that it won't always be like this. It's just that my career has to come first. I think once I've established myself, then I can sit back a bit and get some romance in my life."

Those few occasions when Shaun does date, those rare times when a bit of romance and fun occur in his hectic life, what does he like to do?

An out-going, fun-loving, and gregarious kind of guy, Shaun says, "I like going to parties, dancing, going to movies. I like being with people.

"A great date is going to the beach. I love the beach —actually I love being near the water, even if it's a pool. In the evening, I like to go out to dinner and then see a movie."

He also enjoys good conversation, not just small talk, but earnest, heart to heart talk about things that matter. "If you enjoy being with someone and there isn't anything you want to say, you should feel comfortable not saying anything," he adds. "To make conversation just to be talking is a real downer."

When Shaun has something to say, he will discuss music, aspects of his television show, and his new house. He will also ask searching questions of his date, not to be nosy, but to discover the real person behind the face, the inner personality. He likes finding things out about other people, and doesn't want to spend an evening just discussing himself. To Shaun that would be very boring. He feels that his date should feel that she has as much to offer as he does, whether she's in show business or not. That's why he likes intelligent girls best—they always have something to say that Shaun finds interesting!

Shaun also appreciates a girl who is natural, who says how she feels and is candid about her emotions. If she doesn't like his latest record, he would want her to say so, instead of pretending to like it. If she's turned off by the color of his tie, he would want her to be honest about that too.

Partly because of his hectic career, combining both music and acting, Shaun finds that he's a very spontaneous guy, prone to doing things on the spur of the moment. He would prefer not to make plans many weeks in advance, unless it's for something special like birthday celebration or an anniversary of some sort. He's the type to call you up and ask you out for that evening or perhaps the following evening. If a girl gets upset about this impulsive invitation and feels Shaun is taking her for granted, that wouldn't be true. He just likes to operate that way.

Shaun's an active person on a date, who enjoys indulging in a definite pastime, such as a party, a picnic, or a baseball game. He doesn't like to be idle and would much rather do something with a date than to just sit around. Of course, there are times when he just likes talking, but even that can be done in the midst of other activities.

As much as he has dated, Shaun says, "I haven't met one single girl that I'm all that serious about. I've collected a lot of numbers and I've gotten my own apartment, but most of the time I'm alone. . . . I'm never home when I'm shooting the series. I'm either at the studio very early in the morning or we're shooting until the wee hours of the morning."

Obviously, Shaun is one young man who is not ready to settle down. Not only is he too immersed in his career, but he also feels too young for marriage. As he matures, Shaun continues to shape in his mind the image of the kind of girl he'd like to marry. It would come as no surprise to those who know him, to learn that this image in Shaun's brain is inspired in large part by his own mother, whom he admires and loves very deeply. Shaun is one man who has only words of deepest affection for his famous mother, Shirley Jones. In fact, his closeness with, and his respect for, her has made him realize that marriage and a family is really the one way to be happy.

"There's always been love all around me," he says with a soft smile on his face. "And I think it's prepared me well for the outside world. The only trouble is, it' easy for me to give my affections now, and that in turn means I am very vulnerable and can get hurt easily But that's the price you pay."

Although Shaun's whole life is show business, and he has been surrounded by it all his life, he has strong feelings about marrying an actress. He airs these feelings vehemently, in spite of the fact that he's constantly reminded that his mother is an actress. But he insists that his mother is "one in a million", one who is not very caught up by her career.

"I'd never marry an actress," he has said on many occasions. "That would be the craziest thing for a person in my business to do.

"I don't think it's that great for a husband and wife to have the same position in life. It's not that I would be afraid of competition if that were the case, I just don't feel that it makes for a healthy relationship let alone marriage."

Yet, at other times Shaun acknowledges that "It might be good for the girl I date to be connected in show business in some way. Therefore, she could understand the crazy and long hours I work. But if she were a terrific girl and not in the business, I would be just as happy."

Where he might be lukewarm on the subject of dating an actress, Shaun is very warm about the possibility of dating a fan. He's actually very enthusastic about the idea.

The teen idol, who has had young girls drape themselves on his limousine and tear out his hair for the sake of sheer adoration, says, "Of course!" when asked whether he would date a fan. He is a lot more positive about that issue than he is about dating someone in show business.

Perhaps Shaun's feelings about dating actresses stem from some understanding of what went wrong in his parents' marriage. Both Shirley Jones and Jack Cassidy, at the time of their marriage, were singers and actors. Their careers were constantly compared to one another, often at the expense of one partner. When Shirley won her Oscar, gossip columnists tattled that it looked bad for Jack.

In any case, one thing Shaun is not enthusiastic about, and that's having blind dates. He's not at all eager to be fixed up.

"I hate the idea of blind dates," he declares. "It's just so frightening to think that you're going to meet someone and you don't even know what they look like. I suppose you could get some kind of thrill from not knowing, but how often will that girl be special? I think the odds just have to be against it.

"I've nearly been pushed into blind dates many times but always at the last minute I've chickened out. I think the closest I've got is when a friend tried to pair me up with a girl and I knew that it could end up very embarrassing for everyone concerned. My friend was really sure it would work out well between us but I wasn't so sure. In the end he invited about eight people to his house—including my semi-blind date—and we all had a good time. I didn't go out with the girl because she wasn't my type, but I liked meeting her in those surroundings, with other people around making it easier for us. I know that it probably wouldn't have worked out if we would have been alone."

If you were to make a list of adjectives that would describe the kind of girl Shaun really goes for; the qualifications for the kind of girl that Shaun would eventually marry, the list would include—warm, sincere, domestic, family-oriented, down-to-earth, understanding, affectionate, interesting, sentimental, practical, kind, giving, and helpful.

As far as looks go, Shaun feels that as long as a girl is attractive and pleasant-looking, the specific physical characteristics really don't matter. When Shaun says attractive, he just means a girl who feels good inside, and that makes her glow on the outside. She could be tall or short, blond or brunette, with straight hair, or a frizzy hairdo. Yet, it would not surprise anyone very much, if the girl he eventually settled on had blond hair—just like his mother!

Speaking of Shaun's famous mother, the well-known actress and singer Shirley Jones, what does she have to say on the subject of Shaun and romance?

"Everyone is always asking when Shaun is going to settle down," she says with a hearty chuckle. "That's funny. The poor kid doesn't have enough time to learn his lines, so how can he have time to settle down? Let's just take first things first. Besides, when the time is right, Shaun has promised me that I'll be the first to know."

Who are some of Shaun's frequent escorts? Well he's often dated a cute brunette named Debbie Klinger. He's also close with Gina Martin, crooner Dean Martin's daughter and former pal of Shaun's from Beverly Hills High School. They went to the Ice Capades together. Another girl he's seen out with is Kimberly Beck, an actress who appeared on the "Rich

Man, Poor Man" mini-series. But there's no special or steady.

"I promise marriage won't be for quite a while," he says. "My career is very important to me. I've always been Shirley Jones and Jack Cassidy's kid, along with David Cassidy's brother. Now that I'm just Shaun Cassidy, I'm kind of enjoying it all!"

8

In a world where many teens and young adults are sadly alienated from their parents, separated by bitter words and gulfs of disagreements, the relationship between Shaun and his parents is a unique and touching one. When Shaun speaks of his mother and his late father, tones of deep love and affection swell in his voice. It's obvious that he has tremendous feeling for them, and is very devoted to them.

In fact, Shaun credits his success in part to his parents. "I don't know how well I would have come out of the waiting game to see if I got the role in "The Hardy Boys" if not for my parents," he admits. "They have helped me a great deal in my lifetime and I don't even think they realize it. I just hope that dad always knew it."

In spite of having two people in show business for parents, Shaun grew up in a house filled with love and caring and kindness. He has always felt a great bond with his parents, and with the exception of one fleeting period of rebelliousness, has always gotten on pretty well with them. Especially with his mother, to whom the blond teenager is not only close in looks, but also in spirit. Shaun really loves his mother and admires her a great deal. It's obvious the way his face lights up when she walks into the room or meets him on the set. The link between them is strong and unshakeable.

After all, Shaun, who so closely resembles his mother, was a first child, and first children usually have a special place in their mothers' hearts. Then too, Shaun seemed so much like her, in disposition as well as in features. It was only natural that Shirley Jones should be so drawn to this child who was like a mirror image of herself in so many ways.

Shirley made every effort to strengthen this closeness between her and Shaun. She also tried to be a good mother in every way, even sacrificing her career at times. Whenever she traveled on location, every night that she was away, she took time out to call her boys up and wish them goodnight.

"There has always been love all around me," says Shaun, and he reflects that love in his relationship with his mother. When Shaun speaks of her, his eyes sparkle with affection.

"My mother," he rhapsodizes, with a great rush of emotion in that famous voice," is the greatest mother you can imagine. As big a star as she is, her family has always been more important to her than her career.

"I've had a lot of help," he continues, focusing on his career, "but I guess the person who helped all-round is my mom. She not only taught me all about show business but she helped me keep a level head and my feet on the ground. What she taught me has helped me cope with what success I have and really enjoy it too!"

It was his mother, Shaun insists, who helped shape his perspective about show business, that no matter how much you want a part or a job or a contract, you have to remember that there are other things in life besides work—like family and friends and love, which is always how Shirley felt.

"In my family, we came first, before anything," Shaun boasts.

"I'm lucky," he says, "because I am totally aware of all the sides of show business and my mom is one of the few people I know who's got a complete understanding of it all—because it is a job. I've seen the glory and the easy living and I've also seen the hard work and the disappointments and the ups and the downs."

Immersed as he is now in the world of competitive actresses, some so grasping and fiercely ambitious that they appear capable of doing anything to get ahead, Shaun is very grateful that he has the kind of mother he has. No wonder he proudly claims that his mother is "one in a million."

"I'm very close to my mother," he says simply, his words thick with feeling. It's a feeling that perhaps many boys his age would be too embarrassed to talk about, but not Shaun. He's proud to talk about how much he loves his mother. "She's so family-oriented, it's hard to understand why she went into show business in the first place."

Because of his heritage, because of whom his parents were and whom his half brother is, Shaun explains that he almost feels that it was a matter of predetermined destiny that he become an entertainer.

"This was the way to go. It was all that we were oriented towards, so why depart from a proven formula, unless you dig something else?"

Nevertheless, he confesses that both his parents actively tried to discourage him from becoming an actor or a singer. They knew the hazards and felt that it was too rough a business.

His father, Jack Cassidy, often said to friends of his three boys, "I hope they don't go into this business, because it's so darn unreliable."

His mother would tell anyone who cared to ask— "My feelings are not mixed about Shaun going into show business—I'm against it!"

Shirley always worried about Shaun, and even when he was younger, just a tyke really, she confessed to being overprotective with him.

"Jack says I'm too protective with my older boy," she said back then. "And it's true. I feel worse about things that are happening to him than Shaun himself. There were times when I'd tell Shaun that he couldn't have dessert if he did not eat his vegetables—and then when dessert was served he'd look at me so pleadingly that I'd let him have it after all. Jack said this kind of inconsistency is bad for children; that once you're promised or threatened something, you've got to stick with it. I knew he was right, but it was so hard to change myself."

If Shirley were too lenient, giving in to her feelings and sacrificing discipline at times, she felt, on the other hand, that Jack could be overly strict.

When Shaun was little, Jack, a neat man himself, expected his son to be orderly and neat with his playthings and always pick them up when he was through with them.

"He is a real perfectionist," said Shirley once, many years ago. "Jack disapproves of Shaun leaving toys scattered all over the house. I feel children his age can't be expected to remember. Jack doesn't believe that children should forget what they've been told."

As the years went by, both Shirley and Jack came to a compromise and reached a middle of the road understanding as is common with most parents. She learned to be more strict in matters of discipline, and he learned how to relax his rules and be more lenient. They complemented each other.

Although he strongly favors his mother in looks and some attitudes, Shaun is still a compelling blend of both his parents.

Says his manager, "Shaun's a beautiful blend of both of his parents. He's got the level-headedness of his mom and he's got Jack's wit. He's a true Cassidy. He has Shirley's calmness but he's got an awful lot of Jack's pizzazz and love of show business."

It was a heartbreak for Shaun when his parents, after several trial separations and valiant attempts at reconciliation, finally divorced in 1974. Shaun was only fifteen at the time, but both his mother and father took pains to explain the situation to him carefully. Neither criticized the other in front of the children. Shaun was naturally very upset about the split, but he remained close to both Shirley and Jack and tried to understand.

That's why Shaun says today, "If I'm realistic about this business and know it for what it is, it's because of my parents. They were divorced a couple of years ago, and they were away a lot, but they were always there when I needed them."

Still, the heartbreak left by the divorce was small compared to the tragedy that occurred for Shaun in late 1976. That December, his father died in a fire that swept his apartment. Shaun was understandably badly shaken by the news and still gets upset about it now.

He misses his father a great deal, not only for the closeness between them, but also because he knows how proud and happy his father would be about his success.

"There are so many things I'd like to ask him," he says, somberly. "I never doubted his love. He was a real father. My regret is that he died before he saw me on TV or heard my album."

"One thing about dad, he insisted that I finish school before I went into the business full force. He always told my brother and me how important an education was and that you weren't anything without one. At the time I didn't want to listen, even though I did. . . . Now I look back and really thank my parents for making sure I didn't goof off and did continue my education."

A ring that Shaun wears constantly is a poignant tribute of the love that passed between father and son. The ring is actually a family ring with a special crest engraved on its flat top. The ring has the special emblem of the O'Cassidys who were originally from Ireland. Shaun's great grandparents on his father's side hailed from Ireland but when they came to America they dropped the "O' " to become more Americanized.

Jack Cassidy was always deeply interested and intrigued by his family history. He was delving into his family tree long before the saga of "Roots" made the study of genealogy popular. Shaun shared his love of personal history. Jack was finally able, through his research, to discover what the family crest looked like, which consisted of a fancy seal with a banner, and had it made into several rings. The rings were for his sons, all four of them, himself, his brother, and his brother's children. Actually there were eight rings in all. Jack hoped that his sons would pass the rings down to their sons, and thus the original O'Cassidy heritage would be passed down through the generations.

When David became eighteen, Jack gave him a ring. Now Shaun and his brothers all wear the ring and all are proud of it. Shaun wears his almost constantly, and it reminds him of the very special love he had for his father, a love that persists after his death. It also reminds him of that Irish streak in him and the ways in which he is like his father.

When Shaun was going through the many interviews and the anxiety of trying out for "The Hardy Boys," he recalls how his parents were both very encouraging and supportive towards him. For Shaun, easy-going though he is, it was a very fluttery time. Both his parents, each in their own way, were optimistic for Shaun without putting too much importance on it. They tried to make Shaun be realistic, to make him realize that some parts are won and some are lost.

"When my folks heard that I was up for "The Hardy Boys," they were as excited as I, but didn't build up my hopes. They, like everyone else in this business, have had their share of disappointments. Waiting to find out if you got the role could be a mind blower. . . . But all the time I was waiting, my mother acted very cool. Always telling me if it's meant to be, the part will be mine, that I shouldn't neglect everything else around because of this series."

After Shaun won the part, he discovered that one of the directors knew his mother. The director announced to him one day that, "It's funny I should be directing you. I've been in love with your mother all my life." Without skipping a beat, Shaun replied, "So have I."

Perhaps the incredible closeness between mother and son is one reason Marty Ingels, who would become Shirley's second husband, found it so hard to win Shaun over. It was easier, Marty once said, to get the younger boys, Ryan and Patrick, to accept him— Shaun came around last. But when Shaun did, he was as excited about his mother's marriage and wedding as she was. As a matter of fact, it was Shaun who gave the bride away and escorted her down the aisle.

Like his mother, Shaun put personal life over professional career that night. Shaun had been asked to perform at a special television filming honoring Elizabeth Taylor. It was certainly a triumph that he was selected, but because the assignment would have prevented him from participating in the wedding, Shaun turned it down. It was the kind of decision he knew his mother would have easily made for him.

As Shaun recalls the wedding, which took place last November, "I was a nervous wreck. Mom, as usual, was the Rock of Gibraltar."

According to Shaun, when asked about what he thinks of his mother as a performer, "She's a great entertainer but better than that, she's a super mother.

"I've never looked at my parents as actors. I've respected them as parents. Even though my parents were in show business, their family came first."

Shaun also feels that his family's Hollywood heritage has hurt as much as it has helped. "In lots of cases it opens doors for you, but you leave yourself wide open for raps. Lots of people are anxious to criticize you—they assume you're where you are because of the family strings. It's the thing about having to prove yourself. It's really true. You've got to. You've got to work to be better than average all the time."

Shaun freely admits that the person to whom he's closest, in the whole world, is probably his mother. His friends find that Shirley and Shaun are so much alike, that both are very nice people, unshow-biz-like, very open and straightforward. Kindred spirits, they will say, speaking of mother and son.

About the only thing they don't agree on is music. Shirley, although she dearly loves and respects her son, is still from that earlier day that worshipped crooners like Bing Crosby, John Raitt and Gordon MacRae—the man who costarred with Shirley in her very first movie—*Oklahoma.* She likes the kind of sentimental, old-fashioned songs that she herself once sang as an ingenue on Broadway and in movie musicals.

"I knew he had a certain instinctive talent for acting," observes Shirley, "I don't do the kind of singing he does, so it's all strange to me. I must be honest. It was kind of a shock to me when "Da Doo Ron Ron" made the top 10."

Shaun takes his mother's bewilderment over his musical talents with a shrug of the shoulders, and a loving that's-mothers-for-you attitude.

"Being so much into stuff like *The Sound of Music, Oklahoma* and *The Music Man,* she isn't too crazy about the kind of songs I do. In fact, she told me she couldn't understand why anybody buys my records."

Still, while Bing and John and Gordon will have

always a special place in Shirley's musical preferences, there's no one who can take the place of Shaun in her heart—whether he sings rock 'n' roll or not. As much as he thinks his famous mother is super, so does Shirley think her oldest son is just one fantastic young man.

9

Shaun once confessed in an interview that the question, "What's it like being David Cassidy's brother?" was probably the one that people —interviewers and fans alike—asked him the most.

"I don't get asked that as much anymore—not as much as I used to anyway," he explained. "But it still comes up a lot. I don't mind it though."

The legacy of a show business family and the heritage of so many successful and talented performers has been a formidable shadow hanging over Shaun. Unlike Parker, his costar on "The Hardy Boys," Shaun came from a background where stardom in movies and television was almost a way of life. It was inevitable that once Shaun entered show business, there would be mentions and even comparisons of his work in relation to his parents.

Perhaps the comparisons made most are in regard to Shaun's half brother, David Cassidy. It was David who captured the hearts of millions of teenaged girls and who became one of the most worshipped teen idols in his time, in the early 70s. David occupied the position as god of the teen magazines and universal heartthrob, much like Shaun occupies today. So it is only natural that comparisons and contrasts are made between Shaun and David.

Shaun himself claims that the inevitable comparisons no longer bother him, although he admits that they used to.

"I was afraid of being compared to David when I was younger," he says. "Not really now. I felt like I was not only in his shadow, but in my parents' shadow as well.

"When I was born, everyone knew me as Shirley Jones' and Jack Cassidy's son. When I was a little older and David started happening, I became David Cassidy's little brother. Now I'm coming into my own. . . . They don't think of me as David's brother anymore, although it will always be an acknowledged fact. Especially here in America, they do even less, because David hasn't really been in the spotlight for a long time, and a lot of little kids probably don't even know who he is, unless they watch old "Partridge Family" re-runs."

Shaun was just an impressionable twelve when David debuted in the role of Keith Partridge along with stepmother Shirley Jones in the musically-inspired series called "The Partridge Family," in 1970. Almost overnight, the thin and lanky, angelic-faced David became a hero to teenagers all over the country. His popularity soared and he became the adored hero for his generation. The fan magazines lost interest in the reigning Bobby Sherman and turned to David Cassidy, who graced cover after cover.

David was about twenty-one when this mushrooming stardom occurred, and although he was three years older than Shaun when fame came, the effects were still overwhelming and sometimes even devastating. So devastating that in the end David wound up practically going into hiding to recuperate from the wealth and the fame. Just before he "retired," David had gone on a worldwide tour. In Victoria, Australia, 350 teenagers at his concert were treated for minor injuries or hysteria, and David was dubbed, not at all in jest, a "health hazard." He was mobbed in Japan and Hong Kong also in England, which for David was the last straw.

"My life was miserable," he recalls today, in a candid assessment of what his life was like five years ago as a teen hero. "I had become a freak attraction to the kids. . . . I didn't even have a life anymore. I had hit bottom psychologically. . . .

About his tenure on "The Partridge Family" series, David says, "It was four years on the same set, same faces, same words. It was stagnating," says the guy who was then reaping a lofty six-figure income, not only from his salary, but from a wise investment portfolio.

"A big secret about me was that I never wanted to be a teen idol, for any amount of money. The people handling my career made me into one. I wanted to be a serious rock musician and actor."

Unlike Shaun, who parlayed his concert and singing career into a job as half of "The Hardy Boys" duo, David took the reverse route. He launched his TV superstardom first, then went on to achieve even more fame as a rock and roll singer and musician. Life imitated art, as he went from playing a lead singer in a family rock band on TV to headlining his own concerts in real life. The only son of Jack Cassidy by his first marriage to Evelyn Ward, David made his first records after "The Partridge Family" became a huge small screen hit and established him as a star. Although he held roles before, it was that show which really started him on the road to success.

His first single record, which was introduced on the show, was called "I Think I Love You" and sold an astounding six million copies. With each new record, David fast rose to a position as the undisputed number one teen idol in the country, with some six thousand fan letters arriving each week.

In tandem with the great rush of popularity and stardom, came the toll of his lack of privacy. David found that he was paying a heady price for the throne he occupied. Much like Shaun feels today, David felt that his social life was almost nonexistent. It was a joke, although a painful one, for someone who was regarded as the one guy most young women wanted to go out with, to realize that his dating was practically zero.

"I worked eighteen hours a day, seven days a week," he recalls. David worked on "The Partridge Family" by day, rehearsing and recording at night, and singing at concerts on the weekends. Gradually he began to realize that for all the money he was making, he wasn't enjoying his life. He grew tired of the pace that left him little time to do anything but work and he was exasperated by his lack of privacy; the intrusion of so many people in his life telling him what to do and when to do it. He signed off "The Partridge Family" series when its last episode was taped in February 1974. Then David took his singing abroad, but it was that tragedy-marred concert in England that made him go into retirement almost completely. At the time, he had made several gold singles and seven platinum albums. David was a very rich man.

He gave up public appearances and concerts and set himself down to serious work on music. "Touring has retarded my growth as a human being," he explained.

In November 1976, David bought a home in Hawaii; a balmy retreat that he has always loved. He purchased seventeen beautiful and fine-boned racing horses for breeding there. He decided to devote his time to that and just live a private sort of life. He wanted to write songs and record, away from the public limelight.

During that quiet and secluded time, David was content to stay home much of the time, tend his horses, write his songs, and be introspective; getting his head together after the tumultuous life he had led as a teen idol. He grew up and became wiser in a way that he never would have, had he continued on his mad dash with his career as a rock star. It was during that pause from public life and the spotlight that David fell in love. The object of his affections was a beautiful young actress named Kay Lenz, who had starred on television many times, most notably on the mini-series "Rich Man Poor Man." They had met at a party in Los Angeles in late 1976, and thereafter embarked on a whirlwind courtship.

David wooed her with a $3000 red fox fur coat as a birthday present in March 1977, and actually flew to London where she was working to give it to her.

They were wed on April 3, 1977, at the Little Church of the West in Las Vegas, Nevada. As proof of the closeness between David and Shaun, it was Shaun whom the groom selected to be his best man. Both bride and groom were dressed modishly; David, twenty-six, in a vested suit and open collared shirt, and Kay, twenty-four, in a shoulder-baring white dress with a flounced hem and an embroidered belt. Shaun wore a more traditional pin-striped suit in his role as best man.

Only six people attended the wedding, which David described as "quick, painless and the happiest moment of my life." His mother Evelyn Ward attended, but Shirley Jones, his stepmother, did not. David forgot to bring the marriage license, but the wedding day was saved when a chauffered limousine was dispatched to get it from Cassidy's hotel room.

Nor was that the only prewedding mishap. Shaun and David managed to get locked in the Las Vegas Hilton stairwell. They were trying to avoid taking the elevator down from David's room to Shaun's, but in the process found themselves locked off the floor. As a safety precaution, the management had the stairway doors locked between floors. So Shaun and David were in bathrobes and wound up walking down twenty-four floors in that attire to the lobby.

After the vows were finally exchanged, everything went blissfully. A reception followed, during which the newlyweds officiated in jeans and casual clothes, over champagne and a vegetarian dinner. Then they left for a skiing honeymoon of ten days.

Today, David and his wife Kay live on a beautiful ranch in Santa Barbara, California. David still owns his house on Maui in Hawaii but has decided to resume his career. He made one of his first guest appearances in years on "The Wolfman Jack Show" in Canada, where he attracted one of the largest audiences for that show ever. He starred in a heavy dramatic role for a two-part "Police Story". Then he released a new album, which contained his new hit single called "Gettin' It in the Street" with flip side of "Junked Heart Blues." David feels that the years of working alone have really helped him grow as an artist, and he is now surer of his musical direction and abilities.

Perhaps as proof of his newfound maturity, David is said to be sprouting a few gray hairs. His wife Kay, who's just completed a major picture called *Mean Dog Blues,* says she likes the way David looks with his hair that way; that makes him seem more distinguished.

Whatever happens with the rebirth of his musical career, David will never have to worry about money. He seems to have come through the aftermath of the concerts and survived the trauma of being a teen idol. Financially, he couldn't be better off.

"It didn't turn out all that badly for David," says Ruth Aarons, the manager who guided David, and now Shaun. "He made a lot of money and he invested it very wisely. He lives quietly outside Los Angeles with his beautiful new bride and he's still working on his music."

There is still another important new facet of David's life—helping younger brother Shaun adjust and accept the strange and heady world of teen idoldom. Shaun's lucky, because David had no one with experience to advise him about the pitfalls of stardom at such an early age.

"I don't remember much about David's early career," says Shaun. "But we've talked about what happened to him. If I let things get out of hand, I have no one to blame but myself. . . . I compare notes with David, especially about those hysterical situations where girls are climbing up the sides of buildings to get into your room."

He is extremely close with David and considers him not just a half brother, but an extremely valuable friend.

"I'm very tight with David and I consider him my best friend. I see him a lot and he's given me tons of support. Insights into the recording industry and things like that."

From his long discussions with David, some of which last far into the night and are very frequent, either in person or on the phone, Shaun learned a lot about show business. David told him what to watch out for, what to expect, all the advantages and disadvantages of having success so soon. After all, it's one thing to be rich and famous at forty, even at thirty, but it's quite another thing when you haven't even reached twenty and sitting on top of the mountain. The toll on child and adolescent performers can be deadly. Judy Garland and Mickey Rooney are examples of that.

Having David as a stepbrother who carved out his own special niche in the entertainment world years before Shaun served as another goal for the younger Cassidy—to make himself one of the best and most accomplished performers around. Realizing that there would be contrasts between David and himself, Shaun strove to be good and to fare favorably if comparisons were made. What's more he wanted David to be proud of him. Shaun had the drive to be a star.

One of Shaun's closest friends, David Jolliffe, expresses this drive.

"I'm sure being the brother of a star has something to do with it," remarks Jolliffe, about the success and hard-driven ambition Shaun possesses for so young a performer. "He loves David, but he is definitely a competitive person. He's not an animal about it though. Also, he happens to love the business. . . . He watched David go up and down, and so he knows the pitfalls."

David and Shaun share a strong bond, stronger than most people would think, despite distinct differences between them. The differences may explain why the same kind of fame that overwhelmed David will serve to impel Shaun to seek even greater success.

Simply, Shaun is another type of guy. He definitely likes being in the limelight a lot more than David ever did. He is an outgoing, extroverted person who likes being around other people and doesn't mind crowds. Shaun can more easily shrug off the woes of being a pop idol, such as the lack of privacy and the screaming and tearing girls. That drove David crazy; Shaun takes it with a grain of salt.

David is more of an inward person. He is basically shy and reserved and likes being by himself, with his wife, or a few close friends. It's a case of two different personality types and Shaun's is probably much more suited to the tumultuous demands of being a star.

"He's a private person," comments Shirley Jones, about the stepson who shared starring honors with her on "The Partridge Family."

From the beginning, David, eight years older than Shaun and son of the same father, but a different mother, was there as a guide and mentor for Shaun. Born April 12, 1950, David spent his early years on the east coast, growing up with his mother, then later, when he was 10, he and his mother relocated to Hollywood. His parents had divorced in 1955, and David spent weekends with Jack Cassidy. After Jack's remarriage, to Shirley Jones, this became a second family to David, especially after her sons were born. Shirley really considered David one of her own children, and her young boys thought of him as a brother, not just a halfbrother.

From the first, David was closest to Shaun, perhaps because he was the firstborn and the oldest; definitely because he was the first sibling David ever had. For his part, Shaun looked up to, and admired his older half-brother; the one who showed how to do so many interesting things, who helped him to just become a person.

When David won the part on "The Partridge Family," little Shaun, young as he was, was bursting his buttons with pride. After all, that was his brother up there on the small screen. He actually got more of a kick out of David's appearance on TV than his own mother's. Shaun knew how popular his parents were and sort of understood what it meant to a star on TV and in the movies, but he didn't really appreciate their status. After all, they were older. David was, after all, someone all Shaun's friends could relate to. They idolized him as much as Shaun did.

The days when David was starring on "The Partridge Family" with Shirley Jones were the days that really propelled an even closer relationship between David and Shaun. A relationship that is even stronger and closer today, in spite of the seesaw nature of the fortunes that caused David's star to fall and Shaun's to rise. Then again, David was spending so much time with Shirley and even more time with her sons. Shaun practically worshipped David because he was older and almost grown up, and also because he was a big star. That probably set the wheels of Shaun's mind in motion about going into show business himself. Wouldn't it be neat, he thought, to be a star like David?

David would come over to Shaun's house almost every weekend, and even during the week. He would play baseball and basketball and badminton with his father, then read to Shaun, play with him, and sometimes go to the movies with him. It was David who accompanied Shaun to the very first movie he ever saw, the classic children's story, *Pinocchio*. Shaun was the brother that David never had from his real mother.

During those early years, Shirley Jones would say time and again, "Shaun adores him. Two brothers couldn't be closer. And they look so much alike."

Indeed, even today, as Shaun has matured, there are aspects of his face that remind you of David. Certain pictures of him, profiles, angle shots, look very much like David at that age.

Shirley cemented the closeness between David and Shaun by encouraging David to come over often, and treating him as she would her own son. Sometimes David would even go off on trips with Shirley, Jack, Shaun, and his little brothers. When the brood all posed together, it looked like one big happy family! And so they were.

Shaun was just a budding teenager when David started climbing the ladder of fame, with the aid of "The Partridge Family," but he was intrigued by all the fuss just the same. He started hanging around the set, watching how the actors worked, absorbing all the ingredients that went into the makeup of a television show. He was fascinated by all the aspects of show business. He thought it was fabulous. It wasn't too long before Shaun started pestering his mother to have a part on the show. Shirley was definitely opposed. She didn't want Shaun to appear for even one scene, even one line, because she realized that once he started he'd never want to give it up. She wanted him to have a normal schooling and a normal upbringing. She didn't want Shaun to become a child star.

David was negative about the whole idea too. He thought it wasn't wise for Shaun, who was so young, to get involved with acting. He also told Shaun "no" when his halfbrother pestered him about acting saying that it would be best if he waited until he was older.

"I tried to discourage it a bit," remarks David today. "If you're too young, you miss something in life being a child actor."

Shaun decided that if he couldn't be an actor, he would, following in David's footsteps, concentrate on singing. He formed his own band after learning how to play the guitar and started to sing. He could be just like David, he decided, even if he couldn't become an actor and a TV star.

"It was really just the opposite with me and David," says Shaun. "He considered himself an actor and then with "The Partridge Family" he really got into singing and working as a singer. [David had auditioned for the part after doing shots on "Marcus Welby" and other nighttime shows under the name of David Bruce. He didn't want producers and directors to be influenced one way or another by the fact that he was Jack Cassidy's son and Shirley Jones' stepson.] But with me, the music came first and I feel I've really applied myself to music, and acting is just the frosting on the cake."

After his acting career caught on, David moved to his own apartment. It was further away and David couldn't see as much of Shaun as he used to. Shaun today recalls that time as one of the saddest of his life —that day that his beloved half brother David got his own apartment.

"I felt like crying because I missed him so much," Shaun admits. "And that's a good memory, because it shows how close we were even back then, when I was just eleven years old."

Today, Shaun and David are, like Shaun says, the best of friends. Probably no one understands Shaun better than David, because he's the only one who really knows what Shaun is going through. After all, he's been through it all himself. Both are forging new lives for themselves—Shaun as the new teen idol of this generation, and David as a more mature singer and husband. As much as they differ, so are they alike, and as the months go by, they become even closer. It would be no surprise to anyone when Shaun takes that march down the aisle, if David Cassidy were the one he chose to stand in for him as best man, just like Shaun did for him at his wedding.

Photo by Bob Deutsch

Above: Shaun and Laura Fox appeared at a TV star reception. *Photo by Frank Edwards—Fotos International Left:* Shaun with Jill Jold at the Roxy Theater in Los Angeles. *Photo by Phil Roach— Photoreporters, Inc.*

Shaun and date Marla enjoyed the premiere of *The Rolling Stones* film in Hollywood. *Photo by Frank Edwards—Fotos International*

Present at the first annual Rock Music Awards, were Shaun and friend Robin. *Photo by Frank Edwards—Fotos International*

Shaun and Lori Rodkin were on hand at a charity benefit given by Debbie Reynolds to raise funds to build a museum which will house old movie costumes. *Photos by Frank Edwards—Fotos International*

Debbie Klinger with Shaun. *Photo by Nate Cutler—Globe Photos*

Kimberly Beck and Shaun at La Scala restaurant. *Photo by Ralph Dominguez—Globe Photos*

Shaun with Marty Ingels preparing for Marty's wedding to Shaun's Mom, Shirley Jones. *Photo by Nate Cutler—Globe Photos*

With the program manager of KHJ radio station in Los Angeles. *Photo by Tony Costa—Sygma*

Shaun and Debby Boone at the KHJ Cavalcade of Stars Forum in 1977. *Photo by Audrey Chiu—Michelson Agency*

151

Shaun with Darth Vader of *Star Wars* and Meadowlark Lemon of the Harlem Globetrotters. *Photo by Ralph Dominguez—Globe Photos*

The *Duke* John Wayne meets the pop music *King* Shaun Cassidy. *Photo by Peter Borsari—Camera 5*

Above: With a KHJ radio station disc jockey. *Photo by Tony Costa —Sygma Right:* Shaun is always happy to meet fans and sign autographs for them. *Photo by Bob Noble—Globe Photos*

Shaun's home is a haven of solitude. It's the perfect place to unwind after hectic concert tours and days of shooting "The Hardy Boys". *Photos by Gene Trindl—Globe Photos*

Photo by Gene Trindl—Globe Photos

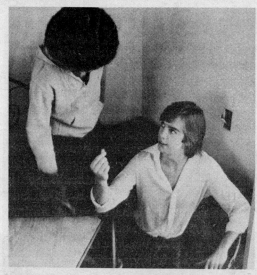

Shaun with his real estate agent and friend. *Photos by Tony Costa —Sygma*

Photo by Audrey Chiu—Michelson Agency

Shaun enjoys spending time with his friends and what better way to relax than go bowling. *Photo by Tony Costa—Sygma*

Bowling is one of Shaun's favorite activities. *Photo by Tony Costa —Sygma*

10

You know him from his weekly appearances as Joe Hardy on the popular "Hardy Boys" TV series; you know him as the sweet-faced singer of hit songs and concerts; and you know him by his famous bloodlines—son of Shirley Jones and the late Jack Cassidy, half brother of David Cassidy. Shaun is just nineteen, an age when most guys are struggling through college or the demands of a first post-high-school job. Although not yet twenty, Shaun is already enjoying the kind of million-dollar success that comes to most show business performers, rarely, if at all. What's more, he has earned the respect and admiration of his fellow performers and co-workers who say, with regularity, that despite the superstar status, Shaun is a regular guy.

What is Shaun Cassidy the person really like? What is the actor-singer-composer and finally teen-idol-supreme all about?

Friends remark on Shaun's modesty and his down-to-earth quality. "He probably inherits that from his mother," says a public relations worker who has known Shaun for a while. "She never pulled that star treatment business ever. And Shaun's like that. It's amazing—the more successful, the more of a teen idol he becomes, the more secure and natural he is. It's hard to believe how unassuming he is, how he doesn't have any of that arrogance or conceit. He has more naturalness than performers with a fraction of his success. Ten-year-old kids of movie stars have shown more stuck up attitudes and snobbishness than he ever would. He's really got a handle on himself and his life."

Shaun possesses a great sense of calm. No matter how hard he's working, no matter how many projects he has to do, he never seems to get frazzled, at least not excessively. Shaun seems to become more relaxed as he gets busier. He juggles the most amazing number of activities very placidly.

Older folks often comment on what a "nice kid" Shaun is, how much they like his company. They say he doesn't display the childish temper tantrums that many young stars do, who find it understandably difficult to handle the demands of a fulltime career at such a tender age. The fact is, that for a long time Shaun hasn't been a kid. Oh sure, he's only nineteen, just emerging into young adulthood, but Shaun possesses a maturity and a wisdom that far outreach his years. It's probably due to his environment, since children of show business performers become attuned to the ways of the world and grow up a lot faster than their counterparts in Ohio or Florida.

Then, too, Shaun has matured through two very sobering influences—the death of his father, when he had to learn to deal with that tragedy as a man, and the teen idol reign of David Cassidy, when he saw all the dreams and the greatness of being a hero collapse into misfortune. He's seen the good and the bad side of stardom and has learned to be philosophical about it all. He realizes that stardom is not an answer but just a means to an end.

"There have been times," Shaun explains soberly, "When I've been in limousines where you couldn't see out the windows because they were completely covered with bodies. Once, they even fell through the roof. I've snuck by crowds by disguising myself as the chauffeur. A few times I've had my hair pulled out until my head bled."

Sounds like a terrible way to make a living. Right? But Shaun just shrugs his shoulders, smiles that dazzling smile and says, "I can't imagine doing anything else. This is all I've known since I was born. Living out of a suitcase and running around a lot. I enjoy living my career instead of preparing for one."

Knowing that the public can be fickle, that idols can plummet from stardom as fast as they rise, Shaun tries to take all of it with a large grain of salt and to just be content that he's riding high now. He vows that stardom will never push him into a never-never land far-removed from reality and secluded from people, the kind of life the late Elvis Presley was forced to lead, hiding from the world in his Memphis home. "I try to cope," declares Shaun, and so he does with all the dizzying effects of his success.

"Right now," he confesses, "I'd be more upset if they didn't go crazy. . . . The trick, I suppose, is not to take it so seriously that it can make me go bonkers. I try to be rational about it. I'm on the upswing now, but I know it can't keep going up indefinitely. And when it starts to go down, I can't let it throw me.

"I'm a realist. I'm very realistic about myself and my own ability. Perhaps too much so for my own good, because, just maybe, I lose some excitement, some of the enthusiasm about some things. I always figure everything out logically: why this may or may not work, why this is good or bad or whatever. I don't live in a fantasy world very often."

Time and again, people who know Shaun well; those who are close to him, declare if ever there was someone who could handle the burden of being a teen idol, it would have to be Shaun Cassidy.

Says one of his best friends, actor David Jolliffe, "Shaun and I have been friends for about three years. We used to go bowling five times a week, play pinball and ping-pong. But it's been getting harder and harder to find the time to goof off. . . . I happen to think he's equipped to handle himself, because he's very much like his mother. . . . He knows the pitfalls too."

As more and more girls pursue and mob him, Cassidy remains, according to Jolliffe, pretty much nonplussed by it all. He's even a little bewildered by all the attention and the fuss. Sometimes he has this air of not believing it's all really happening.

"They've got the wrong guy," he'll say to his friends after an outing during which he was besieged and swooned over by several hundred girls.

Scratching his head and saying in a tone of absolute understatement, and with typical modesty and amazement, "I seem to have an ability to disrupt things."

Shaun does not actively seek out whipping his fans into a frenzy, or driving them to the point of hysteria. That's something he'd rather do without. He considers himself just an average teen who happens to be the current rage. He declares that he never would induce the kind of hyped-up reactions that could be dangerous.

"The question is not whether I'll be able to handle my career emotionally but whether I'll be able to last physically," he says, referring not only to the toll his fans take, but the endless work pace he has set for himself, with concert tours, TV rehearsals and recording sessions. "But I've always been a very conservative person and know my limitations. If things get too crazy and unmanageable, I'll slow down. There's no rush. I plan to be around for a long time."

Perhaps the most telling sign that Shaun will be able to come through his reign as a teen prince with but a few scrapes, is the attitude of his mother, who would indeed fret and worry if she thought that there was something to worry about.

"I guess it had to happen some day," Shirley says, referring to her son's rapid transformation into the hottest star of today. "But he's very responsible and level-headed. Success came to him very quickly. I worried for a while about the effect that it would have on him, but he seems to be handling it very well. He's into the reality of the business and not the fantasy of it."

Shaun displays this level-headedness when he says, "People think I'm being taken for the ride of my life. . . . I am being exploited. But who's the main exploiter? It's me. . . . When you put yourself in show business, you're exploiting yourself. I'm totally aware of all the exploitation that's going on. Whether they're making Hardy Boys tee-shirts or Paul Newman mustaches, if people want to buy that stuff, fine, but I'm not being taken for some big ride."

Since Shaun's phenomenal rise to the top of the current show business stable, his spending has been modest for a star of his stature, who's been offered up to $75,000 for a one-night concert appearance. After a period of several months of househunting, Shaun bought himself a house, a $125,000 bungalow with two bedrooms in Beverly Glen Canyon. It's very rustic and homey, with lots of wood fixtures and stone. He calls it his "log cabin", and it has an electric gate to keep out the ever-increasing number of intrusive fans.

"Very woodsy, very warm, very country-like," he says, describing his house. "I like living alone, although I'm never home. I sleep there, that's all."

Right now, the house doesn't have too much furniture, because Shaun doesn't have that much time to go hunting for decorating supplies. "I keep walking around my mom's house, saying, 'Hmmm, that chair would look good in my living room.'"

The house has an eighteen-foot front yard, with a wooden gate around it where his dog, Sun, a golden retriever romps. The dog was a Christmas present from his mother. There's also a small garage where he keeps his car.

The living room, decorated with early American furniture, has a working fireplace in it. There's also an old roll-top desk and a comfortable couch with two chairs. Shaun made one of the bedrooms into a music room where he does most of his composing. There's a piano, a video tape recorder, and large, beige print pillows on the floor to relax on. The walls are hung with Shaun's gold records. There are red shingles on the roof and a large citrus tree in the front yard. Plus, of course, electronic buzzers to let Shaun know who's outside. Right after he moved, the beginning of last December, some persistent fans found out his address, so he had to install elaborate security measures.

There's also a comfy kitchen in his house, but Shaun, always on the go, says he hardly ever uses it—except maybe to make coffee once in a while.

One of the reasons that Shaun moved out of his mother's house that he shared with his two younger brothers, Patrick and Ryan, was because the site was clearly marked on the maps of celebrity houses that are on sale for tourists to Hollywood. The result was that Shaun found it harder and harder to have any privacy.

Another reason was that Shaun, who has naturally become fully self-supporting, felt that it was time to be on his own. Realizing that at his age most kids in college were living on their own either in off-campus housing or at least in dormitories away from their parents; it was, he believed, time to flee the family nest.

His mother was in complete agreement, and Shaun quips, "My mother thinks that when you are eighteen and on your own, room service should stop."

Besides the house, Shaun hasn't bought many other things or splurged. He did buy a new car; a BMW— the same model that Parker has. Shaun used to drive his mother's 1971 Cadillac around town but found that car much too bulky and heavy for his taste. After considering both a BMW and a Mercedes, he finally decided on the coal black BMW. He loves driving around Hollywood in it and loves having his own car.

Shaun says that there are a lot of preconceived notions about what he is like, and some of them aren't very flattering. Somehow, he feels, people think teen idols aren't very smart.

"People have very strong expectations of what I'm going to be like," he says, displaying that gift of honesty, and adds, "Stupid is a very big expectation. . . . People really expect me to be some kind of yo-yo and have no idea what's going ón. I guess it's because of my age."

Yet Shaun insists to people who express this idea, "I'm having a ball. When I used to travel with David and I saw all the attention he was getting, I thought to myself, 'Boy that's fun.' Now that it's happening to me, I'm loving every minute of it. I love the business and have always wanted to contribute something to it. Now that I'm getting the opportunity, well, it's a terrific feeling.

"A lot of people, when they first meet me, expect me to be much different than I am. They tell me, all the time, that I'm nothing like what they expect me to be . . . and I don't know if it's better or worse. . . . I'm usually not what people expect and they're usually surprised."

Shaun's a gregarious, fun-loving type, who despite any preconceptions, has a lot of raw intelligence. He's very sharp and quick. He's outgoing and knows how to relax in the limelight—something David could never really do. He's also very vulnerable. A sentimental, emotional type, who can often wear his heart on his sleeve, Shaun admits that his feelings can be easily hurt. He's not the type with a tough hide. He's a sensitive and thoughtful person, which may be one reason why he treats his fans so well. Shaun always figures that he would feel terrible if someone snapped at him, so he's always polite—or at least as polite as he can be under the circumstances.

With a grin, he admits that he doesn't mind all the marriage proposals he's been getting lately. He doesn't intend to accept any of them, but he's flattered by the offers.

"I don't know how to react sometimes, but it all adds up to excitement," he exclaims.

Shaun says his best quality is his honesty. That's probably what he likes best about himself, other than his talent. He's just as willing to expound on what he considers his worst trait, and that is "I tend to be too selfish!"

He has a great sense of humor and his friends appreciate his ready quips, especially during times of pressure. He's very quick with a dry, witty remark or a cynical joke.

"I'm more conservative than Shaun," observes Parker Stevenson. "We come from very different backgrounds. What allows us to be close is our differences. We amuse each other."

Other peoole talk about Shaun's wonderful sense of comedy, which they say his father also had. Shaun himself says, "I have an off-the-wall sense of humor. Satire makes me laugh a lot. "Saturday Night Live" on TV makes me laugh. I like comedy that isn't trying to be comedy. I like Mel Brooks movies, but not all kinds of slapstick."

One thing that is very serious to Shaun is his family. He's very much oriented to his mother and his brothers and stops by their house whenever he can, which is often a couple times a week. Shirley will also call her son to see how he is, and if he'd like a casserole or anything. His mother also likes to make sure that Shaun is getting enough rest.

It's no wonder that a guy who is likely to trumpet, "My mom's the greatest," or who claims that David Cassidy is his best friend in the whole world, would be looking forward to starting a family of his own someday. Shaun loves children and want to be a father. That goal is off in the distant future for the time being, but it's something that he has definitely decided that he wants. Sometimes, knowing how great his mother is, he misses not having the kind of special someone with whom he could share what is happening to him right now; with whom he could share these very extraordinary moments in his life. Like his mother, he is an old-fashioned type of guy. Shaun couldn't imagine going through life without a wife and children.

Shaun was never from the breed of spoiled Hollywood kids. His mother, who was always impressed with the homespun values of her own youth, would not have tolerated that. That's probably one of the reasons Shaun has that refreshing, boy-next-door quality. When he was younger and living at home, he was expected, and often volunteered, to help out and do chores around the house. It might be difficult to imagine a star of Shaun's caliber cleaning windows, taking out the garbage, bringing in wood for the fireplace, but that's what he used to do. Even now, when he drops by to see his mother, he often gives her a hand with some task.

What makes him feel glad and happy? Shaun says

it's being able to help a friend, or "going out for a long scenic drive in the country with someone special." Friendship is very important to Shaun and it's something he treasures. He keeps in touch with his friends as often as possible. Fans are also important to him, and he admits that he gets upset because there's no way he can answer all the people who write to him. He knows some of them would like personal replies, but it's really impossible for him to answer all the letters. He still feels badly about it though.

"Trying to talk to all my fans when I know it's impossible" he says, can get him down. Another thing which can depress him is "being with a girl who talks so much I can't get a word in."

Despite his superstar label, Shaun is basically a simple kind of guy who appreciates the simple things in life, like good food, good company, good times. Basically, he's a natural man, who doesn't like frills or ostentation. He can have just as good a time walking on the beach as he can going out to a fancy party.

More than anything else, Shaun cares about feelings and emotions between people. An indication of this is how he filled out a personal ambition blank when he was just fourteen. He wrote that he wanted, to "love and be loved all my life."

What kind of food does he like? For the most part, it's typical American fare, like hamburgers, especially cheeseburgers and milkshakes. He likes to drink Seven-up soda. He's not addicted to junk foods, nor is he into health foods in a big way—just things that taste good—and he considers his tastes pretty much middle-of-the-road.

"I love Polynesian food," he says. "For dinner I

like the Luau Restaurant [he often goes there with his mother and Marty]—where some of the best Polynesian food in California can be had—but I don't have a regular spot. I really don't have any favorite lunch spots, anyplace that serves cheeseburgers is a favorite of mine. Usually when we're filming, we have to stick close to Universal studios where we work so often I just go to the commissary on the lot.

"I have Polynesian food whenever I can, though. I'm also wild about Famous Amos chocolate chip cookies. I'm not sure if they're sold all over the country, so it's possible a lot of people haven't heard of them."

Chocolate is a favorite of Shaun's, and when he's out at a restaurant, he likes to order French chocolate mousse for dessert. He also likes chocolate fondue, the dessert where pieces of fruit and cake are dipped into a bowl of melted chocolate which is kept hot over a flame.

As often as he gets a chance, and that's not too often these days, Shaun likes to do the kinds of things that most teens and young adults like to do—dance, date, laugh, party, go to the beach—during the preciously free moments he has when he's not recording, rehearsing, filming or writing songs.

The summer is probably his favorite time of year, but since California has relatively good, warm weather all year round, Shaun finds that he can go out and enjoy himself almost all the time.

Compared to Parker, who's New York oriented, Shaun is a dyed-in-the-wool Californian. As a matter of fact, on one of his trips to New York, he had nothing warmer than a sweater to wear. Shaun was running around the city with just two mufflers wrapped around his neck and some heavy socks to keep out the cold. Since he's been touring around the country early this year, though, no doubt Shaun has bought a warm, wooly coat for the colder regions.

No matter how many times he's been there, Shaun still enjoys going to Disneyland. It's one of his favorite places in California. He enjoys popping in there on a lazy summer day and just meandering around through all the sights and the rides, exploring the different events. He usually wears sunglasses and a hat when he goes out so that he doesn't get recognized too easily.

Probably on top on his list of outdoor activities is just a very simple outing that many teens enjoy in the summer—spending the day at the beach. Shaun is really a beach nut and would be the first to admit it. He loves to go beachcombing. Impulsive and quick to make a decision, he'll often jump in his car on the spur of the moment and head off to one of the beaches where he'll swim, lie in the sand, listen to music, chat with friends. That's his idea of a wonderful and really relaxing time.

He tans easily, so he never has to worry about getting a bad sunburn. When the sun gets too hot, he'll just zip under an umbrella, usually sipping some cold cola or other soda over ice.

That's why the beach is the best place for Shaun to take a date. He feels he can really relax there and get to know a girl at the same time. There's no artificiality to the situation, like there can be out at a fancy dinner.

"I've always loved the ocean and being raised on the West Coast, I guess you could say I'm a beach boy at heart," he says.

"Another pastime I really enjoy is bowling! Even

when I was on tour in Europe, I found a place to bowl in Amsterdam! It was the same type of bowling we have here except the scoring was different.''

Before Shaun became involved with the many careers he juggles so successfully now, he used to bowl almost every weekday night and then sometimes on the weekends. Now he just doesn't have that much time to go bowling, although he's still been able to keep his score in the 250-280 range on good nights.

Shaun is also a great baseball fan. He used to play on the Little League when he was in junior high school.

"Now I play baseball with a team that Warner Brothers puts together," he says. "My position is left field and I'm a pretty good hitter. I also play tennis but I think of myself as just an average player."

Shaun also likes to go skiing, although now that he does the show, it's too risky for him to indulge himself. He used to love to vacation at his mother's retreat in Big Bear where he often mounted the slopes.

Shaun considers himself a good sport, one who likes to play games for the sake of enjoyment, not just to win. "I think I'm a very good sport. I like winning but I don't get angry when I lose."

Backgammon, a board game, similar to checkers, is another game Shaun enjoys. Sometimes he plays during spare moments on "The Hardy Boys" set.

With his love for the outdoors and sports, it's understandable that Shaun doesn't smoke. He thinks it's an unhealthy habit, and as far as girls who smoke are concerned, he says, "Smoking is a definite turn-off for me."

Going to rock concerts is another activity high on

the list of Shaun's preferences. Although now, with his own successful concert career, it's more likely that he would headline a concert than actually attend one as a spectator. Shaun likes to keep abreast of what's happening in music, as well as just listening to groups he enjoys. He has seen just about every popular rock group of this decade perform live on stage. He would be hard-pressed to name his favorite performer in music, but he's especially partial to Elton John, Led Zeppelin, and Rod Stewart. Although Shaun has never seen him perform, probably Paul McCartney is the artist he admires the most. Shaun's one of those music lovers who likes to listen to old Beatles hits from the 1960s. He also likes the Beach Boys, and is crazy about Bette Midler; he considers himself one of those ardent "Midler freaks."

Shaun loves to dance and finds he can really unwind by going out to a discotheque. He's a fabulous dancer and tries to keep up with all the latest steps. When he was in New York, he made a special trip to the famed dancing spot, Studio 54, which was to him a highlight of his journey. He also goes to Beverly Hills discos as often as he can.

His favorite actors? He'll see any movie with Dustin Hoffman in it, sometimes even twice. He also strongly admires Katharine Hepburn and has dreams of doing a movie someday with another Katharine—Katharine Ross.

He doesn't get too much time to watch TV but usually makes a point of watching "Saturday Night Live," the satire show that airs around 11:30 on Saturday evenings. "It's so funny," says Shaun. "I stay home on Saturday nights just to watch it."

He doesn't have that much time to read, but Shaun really likes to read to keep up with what's going on in the world. He likes magazines better than books, since his time is so limited. He also tries to watch the news every night in case he hasn't had time to glance at a newspaper during the day. Shaun doesn't want to know what's happening just in the entertainment world—he wants to also know what's happening in the other professions and in politics.

Shaun's not a loner type. Far from it. He's a man who really enjoys large groups; being with lots of people. He's the kind who unwinds and relaxes best with a group of people—never the kind of guy who would sit off by himself to work out a problem. Instead, he'd try to forget about it by having fun with some friends. He's very socially minded.

He has a secret wish—that is, he wouldn't mind being invisible. If he could have some kind of supernatural power, it would be to switch into being invisible when he felt like it. Then he'd be able to get the privacy he sometimes craves.

Does Shaun have any fears? Yes, he does, and he's honest enough to admit them. "I don't like walking alone at night too much. That scares me. I'm scared of heights. Flying. Well, I'm not really scared of flying but I don't like it. I fly so much, but if I get really rich someday, maybe I'll buy my own train and use that."

Shaun is an amateur magician. He's always been interested in magic tricks since he was little and used to hold magic shows for kids in his neighborhood.

He doesn't really have too much time for hobbies, outside of playing the guitar and the piano which he usually does while working on songs anyway. "My life is a hobby," he will say, because that's how much he enjoys his career.

He's an animal lover. When he was living at his mother's house, he took care of their family dogs and cats. The menagerie included a schnauzer named Maggie, a Labrador retriever named Cyrano, and two cats called Gemini and Samantha. Now he has his very own pet called Sun, a golden retriever.

Shaun has always been very interested in the study of psychology. If he had more time, he would like to take a course in it.

As far as clothes go, Shaun likes to go casual, mostly wearing sports and leisure clothes. He likes cotton, open-necked sportshirts, usually tailored. When it gets cold, he grabs a pull-over sweater. Even for dressy occasions, you'll find Shaun in a tuxedo with an open-necked shirt. Once in a while, he likes a really freaky, far-out outfit. One of his favorites is a purple, silky number with flowing flared pants and a tunic top—it's a very special look.

He hardly ever wears socks, but prefers to slip into loafers; just barefoot. His favorite scent is Jovan men's cologne, and wears it even on the set.

Shaun's favorite colors are white and brown, and many of his clothes are in those shades. He's also fond of blue, which goes well with his coloring. He's dark blond with hazel eyes. He has a small, lean frame and weighs about 135 pounds, which is on a height of 5'11".

Astrologically Shaun is a Libra, the sign of the scales, which reflects a good bit of his basic attitude towards life—level, steady, methodical, dependable. Librans are known for their tendency to weigh things of importance carefully before making a decision and Shaun does that. They also try to achieve a balance in their lives, which is how Shaun pursues his career—not just exploring acting and singing, but also writing and composing and maybe even producing.

Out of all the terrific experiences Shaun has had in his life, there's still one thing that gets him more excited than anything else. That's the thrill of composing a good song. When he sits down at the piano and puts together a winning melody, he feels on top of the world.

Who are his friends? Well, closest of course is his half brother David, who is always on better and better terms with Shaun as time goes by. He's also tight with Parker Stevenson, his co-star. Then there's David Jolliffe, who used to appear on "Room 222," Todd Fisher, the son of Debbie Reynolds and Eddie Fisher, and some other pals from Beverly Hills High School. When he goes out discothequing, he's often with such platonic girlfriends as Donna Freberg, daughter of satirist Stan Freberg, Carrie Fisher, Todd's sister and the star of *Star Wars*, Gina Martin, Dean's daughter, and country singer Olivia Newton-John. Most of his friends are in show business, or are children of parents in show business. It's not that Shaun prefers it that way, it's just that most of the people he comes in contact with are connected in some way with the entertainment world. Many of his friends are older, because Shaun is so mature for his years.

If Shaun sounds like your average teenager, well, he is. He's very real and that's part of the secret of his appeal. Larger than life actors are no longer what the public likes or wants. Shaun is down-to-earth and very natural—he loves his mother, is close to his brothers, treats his dog well, and is really nice. Stardom couldn't have happened to a more deserving and sweeter guy!

11

Think for a minute. How would you imagine Shaun Cassidy ten years from now? Star of his own weekly variety series? One of the biggest box office draws at the movies? Most sought after singer and composer in the country? Or maybe a husband and a father?

You can let your imagination run wild, because anything is possible for Shaun. As a matter of fact, all of the above possibilities are very probable, since Shaun likes TV, wants to continue working very hard at his music, definitely wants to settle down, marry, and have children, and he will most likely be getting into movies very soon. His future indeed seems unlimited, in whatever area he cares to explore.

There are, however, certain specific goals he has in mind, right now at least. "I'd like to write a musical— sort of like a Broadway musical—and combine a lot of elements into a concept kind of show. That's probably a long time away though, because I really don't have time to write anything else now. I've just written a script for the show and I had to use every spare minute to get that done."

He'd also like to branch out in a completely different area of show business—producing. "I'd like to have my hands in every aspect of a TV show or movie

—which I could do if I were a producer," he reckons.

Sooner or later, depending on what Shaun wants, the movies will discover this up and coming Cassidy. Just like John Travolta made the leap from TV's sweathogs to star of an important film. Shaun can do the same and as well. It's just a question of his getting the right script. He knows what's best for him and he is not going to settle for just any script to get on the large silver screen. It must be the right property. Right now, he's toying with a movie idea that would team him with brunette beauty Jacqueline Bisset; a romance. That certainly would be the kind of thing that Shaun would be perfect for, and he most definitely would get along with his co-star.

In the immediate future though, there is more work to be done for "The Hardy Boys," several specials for NBC (one coming up in the fall), perhaps another United States concert tour, and another album. Shaun is also busy forming his own production company which will develop projects for him and other actors.

There are many decisions for a guy like Shaun to make. The opportunities are vast, and he feels he must be careful to choose the right things. It seems as if every day he must decide, should I do this or that? Will it be good for my career? Somehow, it all seemed so simple when he was just a big music star in Europe and could come home to the States where he was not recognized and lived a private and quiet sort of life. Of course, that was so much less exciting and challenging than the kind of life he's leading now!

What he's determined to do is learn as much about show business as he can and not to rest on today's accomplishments, but try harder for tomorrow's.

That's the way Shaun feels he can be a performer to last through the public's changing tastes and fancies. One thing he vows to concentrate on above all else— that's music—writing, composing, singing, rehearsing. "I'll always write, he promises, "that's my security."

In any case, don't expect Shaun to fade from the scene as did many other teen idols. He is obviously looking forward to many years of entertaining and performing. "There's no rush," he smiles, self-confidently. "I plan to be around for a long time."

VITAL STATISTICS

Real Name: Shaun Paul Cassidy
Birthdate: September 27, 1958
Birthplace: Los Angeles, California
Astrological Sign: Libra
Height: 5'11"
Weight: 135 pounds
Hair: Blond
Eyes: Hazel
Parents: Shirley Jones and Jack Cassidy
Brothers: David Cassidy (half brother), 27, Patrick, 16, Ryan, 12
Sisters: None
Education: Graduated from Beverly Hills High School
Marital Status: Single
Favorite Colors: White and brown
Favorite Foods: Hamburgers, Polynesian food, chocolate chip cookies
Sports: Baseball, bowling, tennis
Hobbies: Playing the piano, listening to music, writing music

First TV Show: The Hardy Boys
First Movie: Born of Water
Address: Universal Studios, 1000 Universal City
Plaza, Universal City, California, 91608
Warner Bros. Records, 2200 Warner Blvd.,
Burbank, California 91510
ABC-TV, 4151 Prospect Avenue, Los Angeles, California 90027